VISUALIZING THE MORAL LIFE

St. Edmund (above) with Abbot of Bury St. Edmunds formerly identified as "Hengham" by inscription and possibly the monk of Bury who was owner of the Macro Manuscript in the fifteenth century. Painted glass, Holy Trinity Church, Long Melford, Suffolk. (Photograph: Royal Commission on the Historical Monuments of England.)

VISUALIZING THE MORAL LIFE

*Medieval Iconography
and the Macro Morality Plays*

CLIFFORD DAVIDSON

AMS PRESS, INC.
New York

Library of Congress Cataloging-in-Publication Data

Davidson, Clifford.
  Visualizing the moral life.

  (AMS studies in the Middle Ages; no. 16)
  Bibliography: p.
  Includes index.
  1. English drama—To 1500—History and criticism.
  2. Morallities, English—History and criticism.
  3. Mankind (Morality play)   4. Castle of perseverance (Morality play)
  5. Wisdom (Morality play)   6. Christian art and symbolism—Medieval,
  500-1500—England. 7. Art and literature—England.   8. Symbolism in
  literature.   I. Title.   II. Series.
  PR643.M7D43   1989   822'.0516   88-47809
  ISBN 0-404-61446-9

All AMS books are printed on acid-free paper that meets the guidelines for performance and durability of the Committee on Production Guidlines for Book Longevity of the Council on Library Resources.

COPYRIGHT © 1989 BY AMS PRESS, INC.
All rights reserved

AMS PRESS
56 East 13th Street
New York, N.Y. 10003, U.S.A.

Manufactured in the United States of America

CONTENTS

Preface ix

Introduction 1

I. *Mankind*: Sowing and Reaping 15

II. *The Castle of Perseverance*: The Iconography of
    Alienation and Reconciliation 47

III. *Wisdom*: The Iconography of Mysticism 83

IV. Life's Terminus and the Morality Drama 113

Notes 131

Index 165

ILLUSTRATIONS

Frontispiece. St. Edmund (above) with Abbot of Bury St. Edmunds formerly identified as "Hengham" by inscription and possibly the monk of Bury who was owner of the Macro Manuscript in the fifteenth century. Painted glass, Holy Trinity Church, Long Melford, Suffolk.

PLATE I

1. Sower and Seed. Painted glass. North Choir Aisle, Canterbury Cathedral.

PLATE II

2. Wife beating husband. Misericord, Chester Cathedral.

3. Demon Fool with limp club before King. Oxford, Bodleian Library MS. Don. d. 85.

4. Fool dances, with King turned away from him to Deity. British Library MS. Harley 2897, fol. 42^v.

PLATE III

5. Adam digs while Eve spins; center, Expulsion of Adam and Eve from Eden. Misericord, Ely Cathedral.

6. Detail of Doom showing Devil with mouth shaped like anus. Painted glass, West Window, Church of St. Mary, Fairford.

PLATE IV

7. Fall of Lucifer. Fallen angels, in process of transformation into Devils. Painted glass, Church of St. Michael, Spurriergate, York.

8. Tutivillus. Bench end, Church of St. Mary the Virgin, Charlton Mackrel, Somerset.

PLATE V

9. Staging diagram for *The Castle of Perseverance*. Macro Manuscript (Folger Shakespeare Library MS. V.a.354).

10. Wise and Foolish Virgins. Painted glass, Church of St. Mary, Melbury Bubb, Dorset.

PLATE VI

11. The Ages of Man. British Library Add. MS. 37,049, fols. 28^v-29^r.

PLATE VII

12. Wheel of Fortune. Wall painting, Rochester Cathedral.

PLATE VIII

13. The Fortified Castle. Master of La Forteresse de la Foy. Vienna, Österreichische Nationalbibliothek, Cod. 2536, fol. 15.

PLATE IX

14. Tree of Vices. Robert de Lisle Psalter. British Library MS. Arundel 83.

PLATE X

15. Attack on Castle defended by Ladies. Ivory Mirror Case. Victoria and Albert Museum.

16. Attack on Castle defended by Ladies. Luttrell Psalter. British Library MS. Add. 42,130, fol. 75^v.

PLATE XI

17. Last Judgment, with Seven Deadly Sins and Corporal Acts of Mercy. Wall painting, Trotton, Sussex.

PLATE XII

18. Souls being carried to Hell by Demons. Painted Glass, West Window, Church of St. Mary, Fairford.

PLATE XIII

19. Wheel of Life. Robert de Lisle Psalter. British Library, MS. Arundel 83, fol. 126^v.

PLATE XIV

20. Synagogue. Font, Church of St. Peter, Southrop, Gloucestershire.

21. Seven Sacraments font showing Absolution. Church of St. Andrew, Westhall, Suffolk.

PLATE XV

22. Death comes for the Bishop, from Dance of Death series. Painted glass, St. Andrew's, Norwich.

23. Death and Everyman. Title page from undated edition of *Everyman* issued by Skot (c.1530).

PLATE XVI

24. The Three Living and the Three Dead. Robert de Lisle Psalter. British Library MS. Arundel 83, fol. 127.

DIAGRAM IN TEXT
(*p. 49*)

Schematic Diagram showing staging of *The Castle of Perseverance*.

PREFACE

The present book had its inception first of all in the excitement felt upon seeing the morality drama staged effectively (e.g., the fine production of *Mankind* by the Poculi Ludique Societas under the direction of David Parry), and yet it seemed to me that more attention might be usefully be focused on the iconographic traditions which initially must have informed this drama. Hence, the experience of seeing the plays staged not only has proved that these are no dully abstract dramas (as allegorical dramas were at one time frequently thought inevitably to be), but also that scholarship owes a debt to them--a debt that requires not only further probing of their structure and allegorical form but also of their iconographic basis. The aim of this book is therefore to provide a study which will prove useful to scholars and practitioners of the theater alike; essentially, it involves an attempt to delineate the visual context in which the plays of the Macro manuscript had their origin and were made to come alive on the fifteenth-century stage.

The study focuses on the Macro moralities--three plays which are bound together in the famous manuscript in the Folger Shakespeare Library in Washington, D.C.--since they represent the major documents for any study of the morality drama in fifteenth-century England. All three plays are conveniently from East Anglia, and each presents different problems with regard to iconographic analysis. Least typical of these plays is *Wisdom*, which partakes of the late medieval mysticism that permeated a substantial segment of English religious life at that time. But even *Mankind* seems not to follow the structure that should be found in a "typical" morality play, if we are to believe the literary handbooks. Nevertheless, it would be dangerous to make any claims concerning what a "typical" fifteenth-century morality play would be since we simply lack enough examples to make such a judgment.

I am grateful to many colleagues and friends who gave

encouragement to me during the writing of this book. Perhaps chief among these initially was John Hopper, who led me to believe that a study of the morality tradition might provide a worthwhile companion to *From Creation to Doom* (1984), my study of the iconography of a mystery cycle. Without his encouragement, the present book probably would not have been begun. Similarly, I owe a debt to Dan Dixon for pressing me to complete the task at a time when I was feeling inundated with other tasks, most importantly perhaps my study of the Middle English saint play, published as an extended essay in *The Saint Play in Medieval Europe* (1986). Natalie Crohn Schmitt, in her article on the characters of the morality play which I was privileged to publish in *Comparative Drama*, stimulated a crystallization of my thinking on certain aspects of this drama. I am also particularly grateful to Robert Potter for his strong encouragement and to Pamela Sheingorn for making many useful suggestions for revision of the original draft, which she kindly read in its entirety. Any faults this book in its final version may have, however, are my responsibility entirely.

Research for this book was supported at a critical stage by a summer research fellowship and grant awarded by Western Michigan University. My department provided sufficient released time from teaching so that the initial draft could be completed. Some support was also extended by the Medieval Institute and the Early Drama, Art, and Music project, while the Medieval Institute's computer also proved invaluable in the final stages of preparing the copy. For their kindnesses, therefore, I wish to thank Otto Gründler and Thomas Seiler. I am grateful to David DeShon, who helped by converting my original computer disks to a form which could be transferred to the Medieval Institute's computer, and to Juleen Audrey Eichinger, who assisted in crucial ways with other computer matters.

I also need to express my gratitude to the following libraries and archives for kindnesses extended during research on this project: the British Library; the Bodleian Library, Oxford; the Hill Monastic Manuscript Library, St. John's University, Collegeville, Minnesota; the University of Michigan Libraries; the Warburg Institute Library, London; the Conway Library, Courtauld Institute,

London; the National Monuments Record (England); the Library of the Victoria and Albert Museum; the University of Chicago Libraries; the University of Minnesota Libraries; the Cistercian Studies Library; and, last but hardly least, the Western Michigan University Libraries, which indeed have given splendid support to my research over more than two decades.

The illustrations which accompany my analysis of the Macro moralities represent what is perhaps an arbitrary sampling of the iconography to which reference is made in the text of this study. In the best of all possible worlds, every item drawn upon to underline an iconographic point would receive illustration, but admittedly such a procedure would be neither practical nor economical. Nevertheless, it is hoped that the examples included in the plates will provide the reader with a sufficient introduction to the iconography to stimulate him or her to further exploration of this field of inquiry. For permission to include photographs utilized in the plates, I am grateful to the Royal Commission on the Historical Monuments of England; the Board of Trustees of the Victoria and Albert Museum; the Folger Shakespeare Library; the Huntington Library; Österreichische Nationalbibliothek, Vienna; the Conway Library of the Courtauld Institute; the Bodleian Library, Oxford; the British Library; D. J. Coby, churchwarden of St. Andrew's, Norwich; Canon Maurice H. Ridgway; and Canon J. H. Armstrong, rector of All Saints, Pavement, York.

INTRODUCTION

In the England of the late Middle Ages, East Anglia was a particularly fertile area for artistic production, both in the visual arts and in such related arts as the drama and theater. Centers of learning and culture such as Norwich and Bury St. Edmunds have, indeed, left permanent monuments that remain to remind us of the great achievements of the fourteenth, fifteenth, and early sixteenth centuries. This region, for example, had been the center for the highly influential school of East Anglian manuscript illumination,[1] and in late medieval times it produced a remarkable style of glass painting that has been thoroughly described by Christopher Woodforde in his book *The Norwich School of Glass-Painting in the Fifteenth Century* (1950). Its stage, known not only through extensive dramatic records[2] but also through a number of extant dramatic texts, including the Digby plays and probably the N-town cycle,[3] certainly must have set this region apart as one of the most theatrically active in the England of the time.

The three morality plays which are the principal subject of this book are among the most famous dramas associated with medieval East Anglia, particularly the region of southwest Suffolk--i.e., the Bury region--and nearby Cambridgeshire. These three plays--*The Castle of Perseverance, Mankind*, and *Wisdom*--were at an early time brought together in a collection which also included other non-dramatic texts but which was mainly recognized as the repository of the plays that became known as the "Macro plays" or "Macro Moralities." They are thus called from the eighteenth-century owner of the manuscript, the Rev. Cox Macro (1683-1767), an antiquary with extensive personal holdings of early manuscripts and other treasures.[4] The fifteenth-century dramas which make up the Macro moralities are actually separate items that originally were bound together rather arbitrarily with the other unrelated items.[5] Only after the plays came into the hands of a

INTRODUCTION

later owner, Hudson Gurney of Keswick Hall in Norfolk, were they separated from the other matter that had been bound with them in the manuscript. Gurney had the plays reordered, again somewhat arbitrarily, and rebound in a blue binding that contained the arms of that gentleman.[6] This manuscript is currently located in the Folger Shakespeare Library where it is known as MS. V.a.354. In spite of the fact that the plays in the manuscript are neither written by a single scribe nor even attributed to a single date, they collectively provide our most important source for the understanding of the fifteenth-century English morality play, and they further explore human life in terms that are susceptible of analysis on the basis of their visual effects and iconography, for they are indeed dramas that are highly visual and that draw strongly upon the iconographic traditions of the English and European practice of the time. It will thus be one of the purposes of this book to address itself to the reconstruction of as much as possible of the context of the late medieval iconography that informed the theater of East Anglia--a theater that included these three examples of the morality drama in its repertory.

Unfortunately, the early history of the Macro plays is unclear. The extant manuscript copies of two of the plays, *Mankind* and *Wisdom*, contain the signature of a monk who identifies himself as Hyngham, possibly the abbot of Bury St. Edmunds from 1474 to 1479 whose likeness (see frontispiece) still remains in painted glass at Long Melford.[7] Internal evidence, including the presence of the East Midland dialect, does not conflict with the theory that all three plays may at one time have been part of the vast library of the monastery of Bury St. Edmunds.[8] The individual plays, each copied by a separate scribe,[9] probably antedated the acquisition of these copies by the monk Hyngham or their possible addition to the library of his monastery. It would seem that only two, *Mankind* and *Wisdom*, could possibly have been copied for Hyngham directly. In contrast to *The Castle of Perseverance*, which is the earliest complete morality play in English, the other two dramas are dated much later in the fifteenth century, with *Mankind* written c.1465-70 and copied very likely in the late 1470's[10] and *Wisdom* written c.1460-63 and copied possibly after 1476.[11]

It would, of course, be desirable to know more about the

INTRODUCTION

genesis of the individual plays in the collection of Macro moralities, but the dramatic records of the region give us little assistance in any attempt to localize early performances or to understand better the conditions of their presentation before audiences in the region. The Bury St. Edmunds location does not retain much by way of significant records of dramatic activity, and indeed the entire area fails to provide evidence of any strong tradition of production focusing on the morality genre.[12] Yet it is important to establish these dramas as written for the stage rather than for reading in the study or library, since principally as staged does such drama present itself to an audience as a visual display that in its time would have been very closely related to the context of the visual arts of its age and its locality.[13]

The theatrical nature of the plays is, to be sure, underlined by the banns and by the stage directions of *The Castle of Perseverance*. This play, if we may believe the banns, was announced as scheduled for one week hence "At . . . on the grene" (l. 134). Though elaborate theories of staging have been developed by Richard Southern which call for a moat and earthenworks of considerable dimensions, this evidence from the banns suggests instead more usual performance on a town green, a location where surely any sensible town officials would hardly have allowed their grass to have been torn up in order to achieve a theater of the type envisioned by Southern,[14] though we cannot rule out performance in an outdoor theater or game place such as existed in East Anglia. The blank space in the manuscript for the name of the town where the play is to be performed has been interpreted as providing for flexible performance at any given town--a hint that traveling players may have been involved in the production. The assumption that morality plays such as those included in the Macro Manuscript were frequent fare offered by traveling players, however, should be greeted with some skepticism because the current systematic examination of dramatic records for all of England has failed to establish any widespread evidence for the production of such drama.[15] It would thus also be misleading to claim plays of this type as typical of East Anglia in the late Middle Ages without further proof to support such an assertion. Nevertheless, the morality genre does merit special attention which

INTRODUCTION

ultimately should indicate the appropriateness of a critical approach that will focus on the visual and iconographic context and on the plays' attempt to make visible and audible the condition of the individual person in all his or her frailty.

Attention to the question of genre, which may be dated to the eighteenth century, has not always seen the visual aspects of the morality drama as crucial or laudable. Indeed, the term 'morality' was invented by the eighteenth-century critics to describe a drama which they felt bridged a gap between allegedly inferior biblical drama produced by "rude mechanicals" and the high art of the Elizabethans.[16] Nevertheless, the Macro plays themselves remained unknown until William Hone's *Ancient Mysteries Described*, published in 1823, made mention of a "dramatic piece in MS. entitled the 'Castle of Good Preservance [sic],' formerly belonging to the late Dr. Cox Macro...."[17] Hone himself had not actually seen the manuscript, as he admitted in his Preface, where he wrote: "To a bibliopolical [sic] friend I am indebted for the notice of the *Castle of Good Preseverance* [sic], which he saw in Dr. Macro's collection."[18] In 1825, however, Thomas Sharp provided a reproduction of the stage diagram of *The Castle of Perseverance* and also transcribed the text that appears on the diagram.[19] In contrast to Hone, Sharp had actually examined the manuscript, though he failed to give any further description of the play, which he identified as "a very curious MS. Mystery or rather Morality (since it partakes largely of the characteristics of the latter class of compositions)...."[20]

The first extended critical notice of the Macro moralities came with John Payne Collier's *History of English Dramatic Poetry to the Time of Shakespeare* (1831), where plot summaries are provided for all three of the plays in a chapter entitled "Manuscript Moral-Plays of the Reign of Henry VI."[21] *Wisdom* is given the title *Mind, Will, and Understanding*, and he accurately notes that "a large fragment" of this play appears also in Digby MS. 133,[22] which likewise is an East Anglian dramatic collection. Unfortunately, Collier had very definite opinions about the morality as a dramatic form, and these prejudices did not allow him to make very good sense out of the Macro plays.[23] "A Moral, or Moral-play," he wrote, "is a drama, the characters of which are allegorical, abstract, or symbolical, and the story of which is intended to convey a lesson for the better conduct of human life."[24] The moralities, additionally, are alleged to have had a role in the development of drama: "It has been shewn, that abstract impersonations by degrees found their way into Miracle-plays, although in their origin they only dramatised certain scriptural events by the characters historically concerned. The change was designed to give Miracle-plays a degree of attractiveness they would not have possessed, if year after year they had been repeated to the same audiences precisely in the same form."[25] Nevertheless, the experiment which was the morality play was, he insisted, a failure since the form was "ill calculated for a popular assembly."[26]

Collier's inability to understand how the morality plays on stage would translate into concrete visual images and into theatrically effective scenes may be seen as the reason for his dismissal of the morality play as "mere allegory and abstraction, unenlivened by mental or personal idiosyncrasy, by varied incident, or by temporary allusion."[27] Indeed, the complex iconography and impressive phenomenological basis (especially their theatrical analysis of perceived experience) of these plays were either ignored or dismissed until fairly recent times; only in the last two decades or so have we had a renewed interest in these plays, which have proved to be much more lively on stage than earlier critics would ever have dreamed. One reason for the long period of critical disapproval of these plays, however, involved the persistent literary opinion which could admit value only grudgingly in work that was labeled *emblematic* or *allegorical*. The tone had already been set in the eighteenth century, as the following comment by Thomas Warton in his *History of English Poetry* (1778) should make clear: "By means of these spectacles [as presented on stage], ideal beings became common and popular objects: and emblematic imagery, which at present is only contemplated by a few retired readers in the obsolete pages of our elder poets, grew familiar to the general eye."[28]

The Macro plays were, of course, both emblematic and allegorical, and as such they are also directed ultimately toward a didactic purpose. As *Mankind* in particular shows, however, these plays are indicative of the tendency of allegorical structures to take

INTRODUCTION

their form in a surprisingly realistic and lively treatment of character.[29] Nevertheless, *Mankind* and the other plays collected in the Macro manuscript remain reviews of the moral life of man who is perceived as placed on this earth with all the weaknesses inherited from the first man, Adam, whose fall he is destined to repeat. Further, the moral life is not disconnected from the physical, for persistence in good or evil is regarded as related to the fragility of man's nature and to his mortality. These plays are thus designed to serve a function which is quite different from the intention that motivated the iconic liturgical drama or the popular devotional plays of the great civic cycles of England. Nevertheless, in spite of their didactic purpose, the morality plays very definitely depart from the kind of technique we would today call "sermonizing."[30] This observation is based, of course, on recent developments in the understanding of the allegorical structure of the plays--an understanding that owes much to Natalie Crohn Schmitt, whose article "The Idea of a Person in the Medieval Morality Plays"[31] contains a sensible reappraisal, and especially to the full-length study of the morality tradition in England by Robert Potter.[32] Crucial to the current re-evaluation is a better appreciation for the medieval way of looking at terms that were then regarded as concrete but which have tended in modern times to be regarded as abstract.

Unfortunately, allegory itself is still liable generally to be defined in literary criticism in an anachronistic manner inconsistent with its use in such medieval plays as *Mankind* and *The Castle of Perseverance*. A handbook definition of 'allegory' is yet likely to identify it as a genre or literary technique that "represents one thing in the guise of another--an abstraction in that of a concrete image"; hence the allegory is influenced in a formative way by "a structure of ideas."[33] The difficulty may be traced to the abandonment of the medieval definition of 'allegory' in the Enlightenment when, as Paul Piehler has commented, "allegory became separated from its function of representing the spiritual world in terms of external phenomena, and concentrated merely on the representation of abstract ideas."[34] The Enlightenment definition of 'allegory' was surely most forcefully and influentially passed on through the *Statesman's Manual* of Coleridge:

INTRODUCTION

> Now an allegory is but a translation of abstract notions into a picture-language, which is itself nothing but an abstraction from objects of the senses; the principal being more worthless even than its phantom proxy, both alike unsubstantial, and the former shapeless to boot. . . . [Allegory involves] but empty echoes which the fancy arbitrarily associates with apparitions of matter, less beautiful but not less shadowy than the sloping orchard or hill-side pasture field seen in the transparent lake below. Alas, for the flocks that are to be led forth to such pastures![35]

Such a definition condemns the allegorical to a very low aesthetic level indeed; at the same time Coleridge strongly defends the aesthetics of the *symbol*, which he regards as conversely partaking "of the reality which it renders intelligible."[36]

The plays in the Macro manuscript, however, simply do not fit Coleridge's literary definition of allegory. These plays may be based in the didactic impulse--an impulse they would seem to share with the York *Pater Noster* play of which even Wycliffites seem to have approved[37]--but they are not therefore the mere working out of abstract ideas about morality. The soul that is separated from the body in *The Castle of Perseverance*, for example, is intended as an absolutely concrete figure about which there was universal agreement.[38] But the Three Enemies of Man--the World, the Flesh, and the Devil--are also real, as are the Seven Deadly Sins--and as represented on stage such figures take on an additional level of reality since they are acted by human actors who make them respond in very human ways.[39]

The Macro moralities therefore represent a species of allegory that embodies iconography as its most essential ingredient. The iconography, which involves traditional elements of symbolism, is further based in phenomenological considerations, particularly in the matter of perceived experience. Additionally, like the art of the Flemish painters, the drama's technique involves the disguising of that which is most true under the *appearance* of realistic figures and realistic scenes.[40] We should not forget that the medieval view of the relationship between the material world and the real was different from what one might expect as a matter of course today. As Panofsky reminds us, for Aquinas the objects of the physical world are "corporeal metaphors of things spiritual."[41] The scenes

INTRODUCTION

of the morality play are, like the paintings of the Flemish masters, saturated with significance and meaning; then, the use of real actors, like the realistic effects achieved in painting through the use of perspective, meant that life could be all the more keenly analyzed on a concrete rather than an abstract level. Such plays are, as Warton apparently realized, akin to the allegorical method of the Renaissance poet Edmund Spenser--a poet who, in the opinion of no less a critic than John Milton, was to be regarded as "a better teacher than *Scotus* or *Aquinas*."[42]

The late medieval allegorical theater indeed not only achieves its didactic purpose very well, but it also presents a type of drama that is to be taken seriously. It is surely proper, then, that the older view of the earliest extant English moralities, which include in addition to the Macro moralities only the fragmentary fourteenth-century *Pride of Life*, Medwall's *Nature* (Parts I and II), and *Everyman*,[43] should have given way in recent years to a more enthusiastic opinion of them. *Mankind*, whose author A. W. Pollard labeled a "miserably poor poet,"[44] has surely seen the greatest alteration in its reputation. The misunderstanding of the allegorical structure and the iconographic meaning of this play led its earlier critics to condemn it as crude and decadent. "*Mankind*," said Roy Mackenzie in 1914, "is remarkable mainly for the coarse jokes and vulgar antics of four rascals [i.e., Mischief, Nought, New-Guise, and Nowadays], like the Imagynacyon and Frewyl of *Hyckescorner*, thinly veiled as personifications. The author is quite conscious of the fact that he is writing a Morality, and takes care to preserve the traditional form and to insist on his moral; but the religious teaching of the play is stilted and unnatural to the last degree, while the mad pranks of Mischeff and his crew are pictured with a zest and unction which must have gone far toward making the play a favorite with those who loved a joke more than a sermon."[45] Hardin Craig, writing more than forty years later, likewise insisted that the play is one "of utmost ignorance and crudity," an unfortunate condition that he regarded as caused by its (presumed) stage history: "The play has apparently been carried on the road for one does not know how long by a low-class company of strolling players, players whose appeal was to the uneducated and the vulgar. It was acted apparently in an inn-yard by a company too small to present it fully, so that it is badly abridged."[46] David Bevington, in his important and sympathetic book *From* Mankind *to Marlowe*, continued to regard *Mankind* as essentially popular drama--indeed as the epitome of popular drama, which was characterized by role doubling that made it appropriate for a small professional troupe of traveling players.[47]

Bevington's analysis of *Mankind*, however, signaled a change in attitude toward it, and Mark Eccles thereafter was able to report that the play is "a better play than critics until recently have recognized," though he too retained the belief that it is a play designed for popular audiences.[48] However, Lawrence Clopper, writing in *Comparative Drama* (1974-75), concluded on the basis of the use of Latin and of other elements that the play would have been more suited to presentation under private auspices than to production in an inn-yard for a popular audience.[49] Hence instead of seeing the play in terms of faulty allegory and mangled revision, Clopper suggests that it actually has a strong moral basis, especially since it joins biting satire to "a moving moral statement."[50]

On the other hand, scholarly analyses of *Mankind* by Paula Neuss and Kathleen Ashley have identified numerous iconographic details of significance in the play and have sought for the sources of its theatrical effectiveness.[51] These sources, according to Neuss, are visual--"the picturable."[52] The visual sources that she studies are those which are most directly associated with what she sees as the "main theme" of *Mankind*--i.e., the theme of Sloth--which she views more or less according to the conventional modern conception of allegory. *Accidia*, or Sloth, is very important in the play,[53] to be sure, but it functions only as one aspect of a dramatic presentation that sets out to represent the condition of postlapsarian man confronted with the inevitable tension that exists between God's offer of mercy and the temptations of the World, the Flesh, and the Devil. Careful attention to the iconography of the play not only will provide insight into the intended audience response but also will demonstrate the manner in which the play's spectacle is designed to impress itself upon an audience.[54] The method of analysis which will be adopted for this play in the chapter devoted to it below will be to focus on the most basic of the iconographic motifs that appear in the play--i.e., the motif that

INTRODUCTION

emerges from the scene which visualizes the character Mankind quite literally attempting to prepare ground to plant seed.

The Castle of Perseverance, which is the longest and without question the most complex of the medieval English moralities, fared much better than *Mankind* with earlier critics, though it remained unpublished and hence unavailable for general study until 1904 when the first Early English Text Society edition of the Macro plays was issued.[55] Pollard's introduction to Furnivall's EETS edition praised the "unity" of the play,[56] and Mackenzie (somewhat patronizingly, to be sure) called it "one of the finest of its class."[57] E. N. S. Thompson praised it as a "model play," though he felt very strongly the drama's shortcomings when judged against the standards of late nineteenth- and early twentieth-century dramatic form.[58] Attention to the play's iconography until recently tended, with some important exceptions, to concentrate on the tradition of Vices vs. Virtues that was established for the West by Prudentius' *Psychomachia*, and indeed this iconographic motif has been thought to be typical of the morality play in general.[59] However, when we examine *The Castle of Perseverance* from the standpoint of its iconography, several motifs emerge which are united only in a dramatic situation that reflects the problems and tensions encountered when one's life is lived in a Christian world.

Wisdom, which like *Mankind* was bound in the Macro manuscript without title, extends the allegorical treatment of the human condition in the direction of mysticism--a direction that would hardly have surprised audiences in East Anglia in the fifteenth century since mystical writings were extremely popular in this region at this time.[60] Pollard curiously remarked that "Intellectually, *Mind, Will, and Understanding* [i.e., *Wisdom*] is a weak play, but is well put together and rounded off, and with the aid of its pretty processions toward the beginning and end, and the ballet of Maintenance, Perjury and Lechery in the Middle, it was probably a great success."[61] Much later, Arnold Williams in his commentary on the play also failed to note its mystical thrust when he remarked on the play's "dependence on scholastic psychology,"[62] nor does Eccles recognize this drama's central structure when he complains that the "play lacks the focus of a single character representing Mankind."[63] The latter also laments that "Wisdom is too intent on teaching moral virtue to have much concern with dramatic virtues," though he admits that the "play is a good show."[64] In an article which is a critical breakthrough, Eugene D. Hill has identified the supreme importance of image theology for our understanding of this play,[65] which more than anything else focuses its allegory on the iconographic center of the Christian faith--i.e., on the image of Christ, who is here presented as the *Logos* or paramount embodiment of Wisdom. Further aspects of the drama's "stage picture" have also been recently surveyed by David Bevington, while Milla Riggio's experimental production of the play in 1984 has been of great benefit in establishing its theatricality.[66]

Potter has described the fifteenth-century moralities as centered about the idea of repentance, the act which in the Christian scheme of things repairs the damage of the Fall of Man.[67] Phenomenologically, man is encouraged by these plays to see his life as wounded and in need of healing, or as unnaturally separated from the sources of all health and well being. Unless there is an acute awareness of the human predicament, life in the world according to the standards of a secular existence may seem good; hence the sweetness of such a life will be shown to be an illusion when the person truly confronts reality. Reality involves, as each of the Macro plays demonstrates, an awareness of the fact that human life is finite. Indeed, the presence of human life also implies its earthly ending and its heavenly (or hellish) reward. Life's end (which is Death), as another morality, *Everyman*, so eloquently demonstrates, tests life itself and provides an emotional and intellectual framework against which existence may be judged. Death, made visible as a recognizable iconographic type and as a figure who spares no man or woman, comes to Everyman to rebuke him in a scene of human agony in which the hero of the play confronts the fact of his going hence from the comfort of this life.[68] Though among the Macro moralities the only play which dramatizes the actual coming of Death is *The Castle of Perseverance*, these plays are nevertheless all permeated with the urgency which man's mortal condition forces upon him. Because of its significance for the entire morality tradition, the iconography of the coming of Death and its use as a dramatic motif will not receive treatment below in the chapter on *The Castle of Perseverance* but instead is reserved for the concluding chapter, where the iconographic context of life's terminus is discussed. Here the usefulness of comparison with the best-known of the English moralities will be obvious, but also it is appropriate to remember that the iconography of Death appears too in the earliest extant fragment of an English morality play, *The Pride of Life*.

The Macro moralities of East Anglia are, then, highly theatrical and sharply visual in nature, but these theatrical and visual elements are driven by phenomenological considerations, especially by the perception of human fragility and mortality that we recognize as typical of the age. The allegorical and phenomenological significance of these plays hence was communicated to audiences in the late Middle Ages through sight as well through words. Indeed, certain visual details are utterly essential to meaning within the context of each play, and for this reason it is crucial that we understand more fully the visual and iconographic milieu out of which this drama sprang. The iconography of each play will thus need to be seen as a vital and organic part of the total stage presentation in the late medieval theater. Recognition of this fact will additionally remind us of recent research in cognition, which provides evidence that knowing is not the result of hearing alone but of the complex interaction of picture and word, either spoken or written.[69]

This book's methodology rests on the idea that the Macro moralities depend for their meaning on their visual aspects as well as on their texts, and that this dependence on sight suggests that a modern audience will benefit greatly from some initiation into the assumptions which lie behind the various scenes and symbols in the plays. The Macro moralities are, as we shall see, steeped in visual lore, much of it commonplace, and in the iconographic traditions that were broadly shared by the later Middle Ages. When analyzing fifteenth-century East Anglian drama, of course, examples from the visual arts which may go the farthest toward illuminating the plays may naturally be expected to come from the same region and the same century. But in the instance of the iconography of the morality plays we are also dealing with an

INTRODUCTION

international cultural phenomenon, and hence it will be found that in certain cases the best illustrations are continental or are from a period either earlier or later than the plays. The iconographic traditions which merge with the allegorical action of these plays need to be seen as traditions which are not always rigidly bound by time and place. Hence, when making reference to the form of the Crucifixion, in one case it will not be amiss to refer to the first extant example in Western art, an ivory carving of c.410 now in the British Museum. It is not a supposition of the methodology adopted in this book that the specific examples of art that are cited should have influenced specific morality plays, or that such works of art were influenced by specific plays. Since we are here treating a common milieu, it seems instead preferable to invoke the useful critical principle of "reciprocal illumination" as defined by F. P. Pickering.[70] When dealing with this drama, we may expect that an example in the arts and an instance in the iconography of the plays thus may each throw light on the other.

It should not be expected, however, that the iconography cited in the following chapters will in each instance directly illuminate the staging of the plays, since the visual context is sometimes implicit in the plays in other ways on the level of their meaning. Thus only some of the iconography is actualized in what Professor Bevington has called the "stage picture," while some is imbedded in the situations and conceptions upon which the plays are structured. The purpose of the book is hence not to reconstruct the staging as such, but rather to define the iconographic elements which informed this drama. Thus it will be possible also to avoid speculation about aspects of staging and performance style that lie beyond the limits of our current knowledge.[71]

The essential problem therefore is that the traditions which passed the theatrical and visual iconography down from generation to generation in the late Middle Ages have largely disappeared in the modern world. What was once commonplace or easily understood is not any longer necessarily recognized even among the learned. Hence it is the task of the present study to provide access to these long-lost iconographic conventions as they inform the East Anglian moralities contained in the Macro manuscript.

I

MANKIND:
SOWING AND REAPING

The surface structure of *Mankind* seems extremely simple. A young man finds the delights of the world more alluring than work, particularly the work normally assigned to a gardener or farmer in the spring of each year--i.e., *literally* tilling the soil with a spade and sowing seed. However, the expected enjoyment among rather boisterous companions will turn out to lead only to personal unhappiness and despair. Nevertheless, there is a way of handling the guilt and anxiety raised by the young man's former life, and this is dramatized at the end of the play. In spite of certain aspects that may not appeal to modern audiences--e.g., the length and tone of Mercy's speeches--*Mankind* is good theater even on the most literal level alone. Though to be sure many questions remain to be solved with regard to the specifics of the staging of the play in the fifteenth century,[1] we seem at first to have here nothing of the complexity encountered in some of the other dramas of the period. But the surface of the play is deceptive in its simplicity, as we begin to understand when we examine the iconographic context of the play and also its use of iconographic tableaux in its staging.

Like the visual arts of the fifteenth century, under the surface there is a wealth of meaning which is communicated through visual detail and through iconographic context. This iconography, of course, must not be seen as an end in itself, but rather as something which, when understood, will mediate between the play's visual tableaux and lively action on the one hand, and the audience watching the play on the other. My purpose here is to examine various aspects of this iconography, much of which will be seen to stand in some relation to the central iconographic tableaux which show the protagonist of the play with spade and seed in hand in preparation for planting along with his subsequent frustration and his abandonment of the task. The allegory, which tells a story of the life of man faced with existential realities and very real temptations, is thus invested with a visual dimension that is indeed a significant factor in the production, for through the *visual* the play is given its form on stage and is made into something that is livelier than mere literary exercise. But traditional iconography which forms the context of the play does not always find its way directly on any literal level into the scene which is perceived by the eye of the member of the audience. Instead, as we shall see, the visual and iconographic context is larger and broader than what is made literally visible on the stage.

The planting of seeds is, of course, a sight that was sufficiently familiar on the English countryside in East Anglia and elsewhere each spring. Further, in the common imagination of the time, such sowing was a process directly associated with another process, that of reaping. "As they sow, so let them reap"[2] is a proverb not only echoed in *Mankind* (l. 180) but also still familiar in the twentieth century. Sowing and reaping, however, have a larger significance in the play (as in the proverb even when it is used today) than reference to rural agricultural practices. Nor should we assume that the utilization of the concepts of sowing and reaping would have made the play more appropriate for rural audiences of farmers than for urbanites in the fifteenth century. This is not, then, merely an attempt to provide a dramatic action that will be appealing simply to rural viewers, especially since we need to recognize that this aspect of the play's plot is further designed to bring to mind the parables told by Christ to describe in exact terms the function of the Christian life. Man's condition, according to the biblical account, ought to be spiritually fertile, though lives are easily diverted into sterility:

> The sower went out to sow his seed. And as he sowed, some fell by the way side, and it was trodden down, and the fowls of the air devoured it. And other some fell upon a rock: and as soon as it was sprung up, it withered away, because it had no moisture.

And other some fell among thorns, and the thorns growing up with it, choked it. And other some fell upon good ground; and being sprung up, yielded fruit a hundredfold. . . .

Now the parable is this: The seed is the word of God. And they by the way side are they that hear; then the devil cometh, and taketh the word out of their heart, lest believing they should be saved. Now they upon the rock, are they who when they hear, receive the word with joy: and these have no roots; for they believe for a while, and in time of temptation, they fall away. And that which fell among thorns, are they who have heard, and going their way, are choked with the cares and riches and pleasures of this life, and yield no fruit. But that on the good ground, are they who in a good and perfect heart, hearing the word, keep it, and bring forth fruit in patience. (*Luke* 8.5-8, 11-15)

This lesson provides the Gospel reading for Sexagesima Sunday in the Sarum rite.[3] At this time in the Church year, preparation for Lent had already begun, and the alleluia along with the *Gloria* and *Te Deum* had ceased to be sung.[4] The words of the Gospel for Sexagesima Sunday are directed toward the hazards of separation from the Creator and the eschatological hope that in the practical theology of the late Middle Ages is given substance through the performance of the Corporal Acts of Mercy.[5]

Though illustrations of parables remain much more rare in the visual arts than representations of scenes from the Infancy and Passion of Christ, the parable of the Sower and the Seed was a popular one and hence received early attention from artists, most notably in glass dated c.1180 in Canterbury Cathedral.[6] In the sixth typological window in the North Choir Aisle of the cathedral, two extant scenes show the Sower and the Seed in prominently placed glass by a workman whom Madeline Caviness has called the Master of the Parable of the Sower. In a restored roundel above, the sower (his head is a replacement), who is casting his seed from his mantle held with his left hand to form a bag, is moving across ground which is infertile and stony, while before him the fowls are busily eating the grains that have fallen where they cannot grow.[7] A second panel, which is square, shows a sower with a basket of seed strapped about his neck and supported with his left hand; with his right hand he scatters seeds over ground which has been properly prepared for their reception (fig. 1). The furrows are marked by lead lines, and the seeds are evenly spaced across the field. While *Mankind* never dramatizes the proper planting of seed, it does place great emphasis on the preparation of the ground, which of course also is a task that is incomplete in the play since the drama visualizes the interruption of the protagonist's work toward tilling the soil preparatory to the actual planting of his bag of seeds.

In *Mankind*, the events necessarily take place in the spring during the planting season--a time which, however, would not set limits for the time of year when this play could have been performed.[8] At line 691, Mischief refers to February as having passed, while at line 809 New-Guise makes mention of "Sent Dauy," presumably St. David, whose feast day in the Sarum calendar is the first day of March.[9] It is also useful to note a connection here with the relatively standard English imagery of the medieval Labors of the Months, which often assign a sowing scene to the month of March, as in the case of the misericords at St. Mary's Church, Ripple, Worcestershire, where this month is represented by a sower.[10] We are hence reminded that on the literal level the play of Mankind reflects events in nature that precede sowing, renewal, and growth, the latter of which would be given further attention in the Church year on the principal rogation day, 25 April--a day marked by processions through the fields for their preservation from failure and for the eventual harvest.[11] That the playwright has more than the literal level in mind, however, is very obvious, and hence the resonance achieved when Mankind begins to prepare the ground for planting by invoking the Trinity-- "In nomine Patris et Filii et Spiritus Sancti" (l. 544)--is highly significant and ironic. It is ironic, of course, because the ground has been tampered with by the demon Titivillus, whose role is to prevent the proper sowing of the seed.

In the parables of the Bible, sowing is further identified closely with reaping, the end of the process which begins with planting. As the Sexagesima Gospel lesson indicates, sowing itself may determine which seeds will grow and reach fruition. There is also the possibility of planting weeds along with (or in place of) the grain. Hence "such as thei haue sowyn, such xall thei repe," as Mercy insists (l. 180)--a proverb that echoes *Luke* 19.21. It is thus inevitable perhaps that the playwright should think in terms of the whole agricultural cycle--harvest as well as planting, reaping and threshing as well as preparing the ground for planting. Early in the play, Mischief's comic assertion that "For a wynter corn-threscher, ser, I haue hyryde" (l. 53) is more than mere slapstick: the separation of the chaff from the wheat in threshing is indeed recognized in Christian theology as analogous to the separation of the good souls from the bad souls at Judgment Day. Relevant here are John the Baptist's words describing Christ as a thresher: "Whose fan is in his hand, and he will thoroughly cleanse his floor and gather his wheat into the barn; but the chaff he will burn with unquenchable fire" (*Matt.* 3.12). "The corn xall be sauyde, the chaffe xall be brente," Mercy explains (l. 43), and at the end of *Mankind* the protagonist must turn away from a life which is as meaningless and empty as chaff, for if he perseveres in it he will terminate in the everlasting bonfire. And thus Mercy earnestly encourages him to "Be repentant here, trust not the owr of deth; thynke on this lessun: 'Ecce nunc tempus acceptabile, ecce nunc dies salutis'" (ll. 865-66). The iconography of corn and chaff is an excellent example to illustrate the manner in which the imagery (if that unfashionable critical word may be used) is linked to the tableaux of the play, for it is the expectation of Mankind that if he does not act in accord with the rules he will indeed be quite literally subject to burning in unquenchable flames, which can only be escaped from through behavior in the present time and through the principle of mercy.

Ironically, a bad job of sowing in the play will nevertheless result in a termination far more joyful than the tortures of the everlasting flames of hell. Such a good outcome in the play is only possible because of the power of Mercy, who is an extension of a divine principle established in history through the Incarnation, Passion, and Crucifixion of Christ. As an allegorical figure--a personification of a quality, *mercy*, regarded as real rather than abstract in its functioning--Mercy is visualized appropriately as a priest, and it has been further plausibly argued that he would have been shown in medieval performances of the play as a Dominican friar.[12] His rather heavily homiletic style with its use of aureate terms would seem to argue for his identification with the Friars Preachers, but more significantly the relationship between Mankind and the clergyman is set forth in terms of the layman and his father confessor who gives him encouragement to turn aside from the temptations of the World, the Flesh, and the Devil. Theologically, then, Mercy acts to open up the way to reconciliation with the Creator; without him, it is clear that Mankind would be lost.

Traditional iconography, however, would have made Mercy feminine, for conventionally this quality was visualized in terms of one of the Four Daughters of God derived from Psalm 84 (85). The words of this psalm are dramatized in *The Castle of Perseverance* where the meeting and reconciliation of the Four Daughters in a scene known as the Parliament of Heaven actually provides a crucial segment of the play, but in *Mankind* the character Mercy merely explains the function of *truth, justice and equity,* and *mercy* (*peace* is not mentioned) in the progress of the soul toward eternity:

> God wyll not make yow preuy onto hys last jugement.
> Justyce and Equite xall be fortyfyid, I wyll not denye.
> Trowthe may not so cruelly procede in hys streyt argument
> But that Mercy schall rewle the mater wythowte contrauersye.
> (ll. 839-42)

The author of *Mankind* nevertheless is not being arbitrary in his depiction of Mercy as a priest performing a crucial hieratic function for Mankind.[13] The iconography of the play directs our attention specifically to a Sacrament--Penance--which makes the reconciliation achieved at the Parliament in Heaven (an event held by medieval theologians to have preceded the Incarnation) available to all men who will penitently believe in the Christian view of reality and do the Corporal Acts of Mercy. Such acts are to be seen as productive, fertile--sowing good deeds among the folk of this world. This emphasis is particularly to be noted in the late medieval period, when the focus shifted away from participation in the Eucharist and toward the practice of Confession as the center of Christian life. The Mass remained obligatory, to be sure, and persons were expected to attend in order to *see* the miraculous transubstantiation which takes place at the altar, but this devotion was unquestionably in many ways subordinated to the auricular confession which would cleanse the heart and make one worthy--a worthiness that would not be separated from good deeds in this world. Yet the connection with the Passion and Crucifixion remained strong, for these events in Christ's life were held not only to provide the basis for sharing the body and blood of Christ in the Mass, but also to establish the principle by which the forgiveness of sins was possible. Mercy cannot be obtained without cost: grace is not free.

At the opening of *Mankind*, the character Mercy carefully sets forth the importance of God's act in sending his Son "to be torn and crucyfyede" (1. 4); in order that fallen mankind might be redeemed, he who made all things out of nothing determined that Christ should serve as man's "remedye" (1. 10). The terminology is significant, for the soteriological function of the Savior is intended to be seen in terms analogous to those which would be used to describe the treatment of a physical illness. In the medieval view of things as reflected in *Mankind*, man is subject to a hereditary disease, original sin, which he has contracted ultimately from his first parents, Adam and Eve; hence he requires the medicine of a purge in order to cleanse and restore himself to spiritual health. Only the spiritually healthy will be able to participate eventually in the reward of heaven, a state in which one's personhood will be glorified. Such healthy souls are commonly compared to the wheat successfully grown for the harvest, now further separated from the tares and chaff, which shall be burned.

The Passion of Christ, which plays such an important role in the Christian process of the redemption of man, thus becomes for Mercy "that blyssyde lauatorye" or place of cleansing (l. 12). He who was sacrificed like a lamb is the source of the "precyose reuer that runnyth from hys wombe" in order that the saints might daily be satisfied (ll. 35-36). Visually, the lavatory is to be identified as the Fountain of Life,[14] illustrated, for example, in an anonymous sixteenth-century painting now in the crypt of the cathedral at Ghent, Belgium. In this painting, Christ with his cross stands in a fountain, while the blood which flows from him issues through it to become the source of refreshment for those who wash their hands in it and drink it. In other examples, people also bathe in the fountain filled with precious blood.[15] This blood is, of course, God's gift of sustenance and medicine to preserve men and women at the Last Judgment[16]--a sentiment echoed in *Mankind* (l. 35). Christ himself is the Fountain or Well of Life, the source through which the human spirit is nourished and given healing even unto everlasting life. Without this source of liquid sustenance, the seed that is planted cannot spring to life, for Christ in this context represents the ongoing creative power that informs the universe. Alienation from this source--i.e., from Christ--is therefore to be recognized as fatally dangerous to one's health and well being. Sin, Mercy explains to Mankind later in the play, is a wound which should be cured through "surgery" without delay, since "yf yt procede ouyrlong, yt ys cawse of gret grewans" (ll. 857-58). Repentance means to be cleansed and healed in the "precyose reuer" of Christ's blood--a stream which flows from the Fountain of Life.

But purification cannot be simply a personal event set apart from the body of the Church and from the responsibility of the individual acting in the world. For the context of this statement, which is extremely important for our interpretation of *Mankind*, it is necessary to look outside the text of the play for the late medieval understanding of the responsibilities expected of the individual Christian. Such responsibilities are indeed usefully designated in the sermon for Sexagesima Sunday in the *Speculum Sacerdotale*, which reminds people that the Seven Corporal Acts of Mercy are given to the members of the Church for "solace."[17] These Acts are the ones delineated in *Matthew* 25.34-46--"to fede the hungrie, to yeue drynke to the thristie, to visite the seke, to clothe the nakyd, poore men and pilgrymmes for to herborwy, for to go to the prisoners"--as obligatory if the person is not to be turned away at the Last Day, and in addition a seventh, "to berye the dede," from *Tobit*.[18] "These are yeven vnto this spouse [i.e., the Church] for to be holden with hure that she may by the obseruaunce of hem and of the commaundmentis of God haue opyned to hure the gate of hure spouse and lord and gladly halse or bicleppe hym."[19] The

Savior, says Mercy in *Mankind*, is like "to a lambe" (l. 34) which, as may be observed in the instance of the Mystic Lamb in Jan van Eyck's well-known *Adoration of the Mystic Lamb*, is at once the object of devotion and the source of happiness and spiritual health. The blood spilled in Christ's sacrifice is, Mercy explains, of a potency that will dissolve the bond which unites Mankind to his "mortall enmye, that vemynousse serpente" (ll. 39-40). To release one from such bonds is, according to the orthodox teaching of the Church, the proper task of the clergy, whose role in this instance involves the ability to bind and loose sin--the power of the keys delegated through St. Peter.[20] But to be freed from sin and guilt is also to be released from a bondage to the self that would prevent the performance of the Seven Corporal Acts of Mercy. It is, then, no accident that the Seven Corporal Acts are thus noted in the sermon in the *Speculum Sacerdotale* for Sexagesima Sunday, the same day for which the Gospel reading of the Sower and the Seed was designated in the Sarum rite.

Within this earthly life, however, no one should expect to be freed from the assaults of the World, the Flesh, and the Devil--the Three Enemies of Man--who receive increasing attention in Christian thought beginning with the twelfth century.[21] After Mankind has failed at the task assigned him--a failure that has been effected through the external influence of the devil Titivillus--Mercy provides the following explanation of what has happened:

> Ye hawe thre aduersaryis and he ys mayster of hem all:
>   That ys to sey, the Dewell, the World, the Flesch and the Fell.
> The New Gyse, Nowadayis, Nowgth, the World we may hem
>   call;
> And propyrly Titiuillus syngnyfyth the Fend of helle;
>
> The Flesch, that ys the vnclene concupissens of your body.
>   These be your thre gostly enmyis, in whom ye hawe put your
>   confidens.
> Thei browt yow to Myscheffe to conclude your temporall glory,
>   As yt hath be schewyd before this worcheppyl audiens.
>   (ll. 883-90)

Emphasis on the Three Enemies of Man is, as Siegfried Wenzel has demonstrated, distinctly late medieval, especially following the use of this commonplace by St. Bernard and Hugh of St.-Victor.[22] Though Hugh's use of military imagery is perhaps of slightly less significance for our understanding of *Mankind* than for our appreciation of certain aspects of other morality and miracle plays, it is still utterly crucial to note his linking of the Enemies of Man with the Christian warfare established in the writings of St. Paul: "The devil arrays his troops of evil suggestions against the faithful soul. The world leads forth good and bad fortune (*prospera et adversa*) to overcome us. And the flesh rises in battle against us by rousing the hosts of carnal desires."[23]

The Three Enemies of Man appear as the captains who oversee the Seven Deadly Sins in the play of *Mary Magdalene* in the Digby Manuscript--a drama which was written later than *Mankind* and which has been identified as sharing something of its structure with the morality dramas.[24] In *Mary Magdalene*, Pride and Covetousness attend the World, while the Prince of Devils enters with Wrath and Envy; the King of Flesh appears with Sloth, Gluttony, and Lechery.[25] Thus the anonymous author of the Digby play is able to unite the Three Enemies of Man with the *psychomachia* theme, which sets the Virtues and Vices in opposition to each other. As has been noted above, the theme is one that was firmly established in tradition by the *Psychomachia* of Prudentius and that remained popular in the visual arts through the Middle Ages.[26] The *psychomachia* theme with the Vices arrayed under the World, the Flesh, and the Devil, however, had been used already in an extant English morality play in *The Castle of Perseverance*, which dates from earlier in the fifteenth century. In *Mankind*, this theme is used selectively and with modification--for example, among the captains of the Vices only the Devil appears as a literal character in the play--in order to establish a unique dramatic conflict of unusual liveliness.

In spite of the lack in the play of any character who is actually named "World" or "Mundus," the emphasis in *Mankind* seems especially focused on the sins associated with this category, though these are to be sure less strictly defined than in the Digby *Mary Magdalene* or *The Castle of Perseverance*. The role of the devil, Titivillus, while crucial, is much smaller than the roles of Nought,

MANKIND

New-Guise, Nowadays, and Mischief. Thus, although Nought, New-Guise, and Nowadays are especially associated with the selfish concerns of this world, they do not treat the sins of pride and covetousness in any direct or didactic way. The characters are allowed by the author to have an existence that is independent of abstract concepts, and hence they reflect the actual involvement of individuals in lives that are mindlessly empty in their concerns. Nevertheless, they are not in fact cut off from the mental fixation on self that we would define as pride, or from desire for worldly wealth that would enable persons to dress aristocratically and fashionably. In the end, their motives involve them in a life of *game* that emphasizes dancing, idleness, and other actions which, when detached from a recreative release from a workaday existence, close them in upon themselves. On the one hand they must represent ultimately the sterility that comes of their denial of the source of all goodness and fertility--i.e., of the nature of the Creation itself--while on the other they dramatize the effects of a life of mindless and absurd activities. Such, then, is the basis of their dramatic effectiveness, which shares something with the effectiveness of the torturers in the plays that treat the Passion in the English cycle drama (e.g., the Towneley *Coliphizacio*) who likewise are unable to understand the stupidity of what they are doing. When these characters in *Mankind* are in pain as a result of a blow, they further share a mental attitude with the sculpture showing a man with a thorn in his foot in a capital at Wells Cathedral.[27] In the sculpture at Wells, the man lifts his foot to attempt to pull out the thorn; his face is numb with pain, while his eyes, which stare out into space, fail to focus on anything. The principle involved here is one that should have been kept very much in the forefront of any early production of the play, which seems to call for playing Nought, New-Guise, and Nowadays as characters that lack any sense of focus in their lives or actions other than their devotion to self--a devotion which is directly opposed to that promoted by the character Mercy, who in fact functions in the drama as a point of theological as well as theatrical focus for the audience.

Nought, New-Guise, and Nowadays principally are unable to keep in mind their end. Just as they have no respect for the process of planting seed--essential if grain is to be grown and the population is to be fed and not to starve--so also they have no intellectual grasp of the nature of ultimate reality as perceived in the Christian scheme of things.[28] As Mercy accurately notes, their "dysporte and behauour" prove that "Ther joy ande delyte ys in derysyon/ Of her owyn Cryste to hys dyshonur" (ll. 167-69). We may at first feel that Mercy is overstating the case when he claims that this kind of life "ys wers than ony felony or treson" ("How may yt be excusyde befor the Justyce of all,/ When for euery ydyll worde we must yelde a reson?") (ll. 171-73), but quite quickly we learn that this judgment upon Nought, New-Guise, and Nowadays is correct. Their behavior extends to the quality of mischief, which is personified and thus literalized in the character of Mischief in the play. As the *Oxford English Dictionary* indicates, the word 'mischief' in the fifteenth century meant evil-doing, misfortune, distress, calamity; it was, therefore, a stronger word than at present, when it might denote the kind of minor trouble into which a child may get himself or herself. The audience watching *Mankind* does not take long to discover that Mischief and his unstable companions are insufferable ruffians.[29]

Of these characters, Nought seems the most carefully delineated, for he appears to be quite literally depicted as a fool. He is called a fool by Nowadays at line 140: "Who spake to the, foll? thou art not wyse." Then at lines 273-75, Nought himself says, "I loue well to make mery./ I haue be sethen wyth the comyn tapster of Bury/ And pleyde so longe the foll that I am ewyn wery. . . ." It may be suggested therefore that Nought would be dressed in a costume appropriate for the fool--a contrast with the merely foolishly fashionable dress of New-Guise and Nowadays--and that he might even hold the fool stick, bladder, and/or bauble (see fig. 3) normally associated with such a role.[30] By the fifteenth century, the fool in the visual arts normally wore a headdress with ass's ears and a costume of various colors with perhaps bells attached. A dancing fool appears in a misericord of c.1330 in the cathedral at Chicester[31] and in an illustration in a psalter from the fourteenth century (British Library Harley MS. 2897, fol. 42v; see fig. 4); three dancing fools also appear on a misericord of 1520 in Beverley Minster.[32] We are thus reminded that Nought first appears in

MANKIND

the play of *Mankind* in a dancing scene with perhaps minstrels playing bagpipes.[33] Further, not inappropriately, in other examples from the visual arts the fool may appear as a devil-fool[34]--a connection that would seem likewise to be implicit in *Mankind*, though there is no evidence that this coupling was given visible illustration in the play.

In the visual arts, the fool was, however, most commonly represented in miniatures accompanying Psalms 13 (14) and 52 (53) in medieval psalters.[35] It has been noted that the fool in these illustrations "is not so much stupid as a denier of God--a man who uses foolishness as a cloak to further his impiety."[36] Such is true likewise in the case of Nought in *Mankind*, for his foolishness truly involves "derision" which is as deliberately impious as his cohorts' words and actions.

Further attention to English psalter illustrations, particularly those originating earlier in the same general region of England that also later produced *Mankind*, will also throw light on the character of Nought. The fifty-second psalm, like the thirteenth, begins with the words "Dixit inspiens in corde suo: Non est Deus" ("The fool said in his heart: 'There is no God'"). In fourteenth-century psalters from East Anglia, the most common illustration for Psalm 52 (53) shows a fool with a king, but some interesting variations of this scene also occur. In the Peterborough Psalter (fol. 41), for example, the fool appears on the left, and on the right is the king, seated and with legs crossed while he is plunging a sword into his heart.[37] In Oxford, Sidney Sussex College MS. 76, the fool is the one committing suicide--the logical conclusion, as the play of *Mankind* will also show, of a life separated from belief in God and from sincere religious practice. Less usual is the illustration for this psalm in the Ormesby Psalter (Bodeian Library MS. Douce 366), for here is shown the Temptation of Christ--i.e., the pattern of successful resistance to temptation of the type that Mankind experiences in the play. Christ in his patience stands in remarkable contrast to the usual depiction of the fool, who is one that is invariably off-balance. The illuminator of the Barlow Psalter thus has placed the fool, who is wearing only a hood but is covering his genitals with his left hand, actually below and outside the initial which contains the king (fol. 67). The fool reaches with his other hand to hold his fool stick with bladder up toward the seated royal figure, who as in the Peterborough Psalter is committing suicide--in this case, he has thrust his sword completely through his chest.[38]

Lack of balance and of a sense of proportion is also present not only in the character of Nought but also in the characters of New-Guise, Nowadays, and Mischief. As eavesdroppers, they are unmoved by Mercy's quotation of the proverb "Mesure ys tresure" (l. 237),[39] nor do they take heed when they overhear his saying "be ware of excesse" (l. 238). Mercy carefully explains to Mankind that he must learn a lesson from the example of the horse, which must not be too well fed if he is to be obedient to his owner: "Yf he be fede ouerwell he wyll dysobey/ Ande in happe cast his master in the myre" (ll. 243-44).[40] New-Guise reacts to the statement of this ascetic idea with a remark about his wife: "Ye sey trew, ser, ye are no faytour./ I haue fede my wyff so well tyll sche ys my master" (ll. 245-46). He shows that he has wounds where she has struck him--on his head and genitals! "Ande my wyf were yowr hors," he says, "sche wolde yow all to-banne [i.e., curse]" (l. 249).

At lines 135-38, we have already learned that Nowadays too has had a domestic squabble with his wife:

Also I haue a wyf, her name ys Rachell;
Betuyx her and me was a gret batell;
Ande fayn of yow wolde here tell
    Who was the most master.

It is when Nought impudently answers, "Thy wyf Rachell, I dare ley twenti lyse" (l. 139), that Nowadays reminds him that he is a fool and invites him, with a gesture presumably, to kiss his "fundamentum" (l. 142).[41] The trouble of New-Guise and Nowadays with their wives is iconographically significant, since their domestic squabbles are related to the popular representations of such fighting between husband and wife in the visual arts, especially in wood carvings where it is usually part of the comedy to see the husband getting the worst of the domestic battle. A well-known example is the misericord in Henry VII's Chapel, Westminster Abbey, where a woman is beating a man, who has fallen; she holds a distaff. At the left is a fool, wearing a headdress with ass's ears.[42] At Fairford, Gloucestershire, another misericord shows a woman pulling her husband's hair and beating him with a wooden scoop, while at Chester Cathedral the woodcarver has represented a woman grasping the man by his hood and hitting him with an unidentified household implement (fig. 2).[43]

Scenes of domestic violence are indicative of more than mere antifeminism in drama or art,[44] and thus are illustrative of the kind of disharmony that is disruptive to the social order at its very core. If "Mesure is tresure," then the wives of the would-be fashionably dressed gallants, New-Guise and Nowadays, serve like their husbands to break down that which is most important in life--a harmony that is in tune with the order of the Creation and with the principles established in the parable of the Sower and the Seed.

From the standpoint of the iconography of the play, the figure that is most exactly set off against the lack of harmony represented by Nowadays, New-Guise, and their companions is Mankind himself as he digs with a spade--a pose that also returns us to the Sower and the Seed motif though, as we shall see, it also has other resonances of meaning. Mankind is here, as noted above, literally performing a function with a very profound meaning for our understanding of the spiritual life, but he is also symbolically re-enacting the posture and acts of Adam following his expulsion from the Garden of Eden.[45] The biblical account of the earliest age of the world's history explains that, following the Expulsion from the Garden, the Creator condemned Adam to hard labor by the "sweat" of his brow; mankind's first parents must work the soil from which he was given life at his creation ("out of which thou wast taken: for dust thou art, and into dust thou shalt return") (*Genesis* 3.17-23). In medieval iconography, Adam following the Expulsion is therefore pictured with either mattock or spade, tilling the soil as in the famous early painted glass in the North Choir Clerestory of Canterbury Cathedral.[46] In the influential Canterbury glass, he appears with long hair and nude to the waist, with a loincloth of skins; he grasps the handle of the spade with his hands and pushes it into the ground with his left foot, which is bare. Even the placement of this window in the cathedral has implications for the later morality play of *Mankind*, for the glass which illustrates Adam's punishment for his crime appears on the north or *dark* side of the cathedral, while in the south window immediately across from Adam are the figures of the Blessed Virgin and her Son, who represent the coming of light to humankind.[47] Adam's work of digging in the soil is thus at once a sign of the Fall and also an emblem of hope because of his implied submission to his Maker--a submission which will eventually lead to his salvation.

The iconography of Adam digging remained highly popular through the Middle Ages, and appears along with the Expulsion on a misericord (fig. 5) in Ely Cathedral: here Adam, who is digging, is accompanied by a son, while the other side of the misericord shows Eve, who is spinning (a cat that also appears in the scene plays with her yarn).[48] In the fourteenth-century *Holkham Bible Picture Book*, which was illuminated either in East Anglia or in London, the illustration of the Expulsion is followed by an entire miniature given over to the angel guarding Eden's gate, above, and Adam digging while Eve spins, below (fol. 4v);[49] this unusual representation, however, shows both Adam and Eve entirely nude as they set about their tasks. We know that Mankind in the play would have been dressed conventionally--more, therefore, like the Adam illustrated on the misericord at Ely, where he wears a gown that reaches below his knees.

Mankind's opening lines in the play point back to the experience of the first male parent of the race as well as to a direct connection between the human condition and the manner in which seeds planted in the ground grow (and, we might add, eventually mature and bring forth fruit):

> Of the erth and of the cley we haue owr propagacyon.
> By the prouydens of Gode thus be we deryvatt. . . .
>
> (ll. 186-87)

Now, however, because of the Fall he recommends participation in the processes of nature in order to "mortyfye owr carnall condycyon" (ll. 190-91). Submission to God's "provycyon" (l. 193) is hence essential for every person who wishes to enjoy his mercy now in this life and at the Last Day. Mankind, with his spade in his hand and setting out to plant seed, will first of all identify himself with Adam at the same time that he also will identify himself with the positive creative processes of nature. Yet Mankind recognizes in himself from the first the potential for rebellion:

> My name ys Mankynde. I haue my composycyon
> Of a body and of a soull, of condycyon contrarye.
> Betwyx them tweyn ys a grett dyvisyon;
> He that xulde be subjecte, now he hath the victory.
>
> (ll. 194-97)

When the flesh is in the ascendancy over the soul, Mankind laments, one's predicament is analogous to the situation in the family where the wife is master (ll. 199-200), a condition implied by the iconography of domestic squabbles as reported by New-Guise and Nowadays. To obtain control for the soul over against the body, he prays for help to Our Lady and seeks out Mercy, whom he recognizes as his spiritual father. "My body wyth my soull ys euer querulose," he complains; "I prey yow, for sent charyte, of yowr supportacyon" (ll. 211-12). Displaying his inherited unsteadiness or instability--qualities which mirror the very essence of a character such as Nought, for instance--Mankind begs for spiritual comfort from Mercy in the latter's priestly role. He thus seeks for resolution to the body-soul debate within himself. In order to succeed in his quest for stability and harmony, however, Mankind must perform the work himself; as Mercy advises, "Do truly yowr labure and kepe yowr halyday" (l. 300). Mankind must be God's "seruante" (l. 280).

In his obedience and service to his Creator, Mankind must also be patient, and it is of course in this regard that he fails when confronted with the frustrations presented by the rowdy companions and, especially, by Titivillus. Encountering with his spade the board which Titivillus has placed in the ground, Mankind angrily insists that he will plant his seed in untilled soil, whereupon he then further shows his impatience upon the loss of his seed, which Titivillus has also stolen from him (ll. 545-48). Earlier, in attempting to conquer his flesh, Mankind had seated himself and had written on a paper the words "Memento, homo, quod cinis es et in cinerem reuerteris" (l. 321)--an important sentence from the Ash Wednesday liturgy and also a line reminiscent of *Job* 34.15.[50] Additionally, marking himself as a Christian knight, he indicated that he bore "on my bryst the bagge of myn armys" (l. 322); like Spenser's Red Crosse Knight in *The Faerie Queene*, he exhibited the emblem of the cross upon his own body. In his effort to bear his adversities patiently in the segment of the play to follow, however, Mankind will fail in his attempt to be patient--i.e., to emulate the principal virtue of Job. This failure will be the basis for much of the action of the remainder of the play. But it is important to identify here the full significance of Job as providing an iconographic context against which we may better interpret Mankind's response to the tempters who assail him.

As a figure representing patience, Job commonly appeared in medieval theology and iconography from at least the time of St. Gregory the Great, who made particular note of this quality in his extended writings on the book of *Job*.[51] But the identification between Job and patience is older, having been established by Tertullian and later linked with the *Psychomachia* of Prudentius.[52] A ninth-century manuscript of the latter work shows Patience taking Job by the forearm and drawing him through the battle lines, and also illustrates Job and Patience seated side by side above the clash of Virtues and Vices.[53] Later illustrations showing Job also often present him afflicted with his irritating and painful illness. Sometimes he is pictured with his wife or in conversation with his friends, who attempt to reason with him.[54]

That the author of *Mankind* indeed had the story of Job in mind as he was writing the play seems clear,[55] for Mankind is advised to "Se the grett pacyence of Job in tribulacyon" (l. 286). The protagonist of the play is tested in a manner reminiscent of this Old Testament hero of faith. Of course, Job successfully presents himself as an exemplar of patience, whereas, as noted above, Mankind fails, for he is not a saint but an average man. In *Mankind*, patience is an ideal which the protagonist cannot reach. "Vita hominis est milicia super terram," says Mercy (l. 228), quoting from *Job* 7.1; yet, in the conflict Mankind is certainly far less than perfect in the battle against temptation.

From the standpoint of the iconography of the story of Job, its most commonly illustrated feature is the dunghill upon which Job sits.[56] It is perhaps useful to recognize that there is a phenomenological connection between the dunghill--i.e., refuse which is the opposite of food, and yet the resulting end-product of eating such food--and the sowing of seed in the ground in order to produce food at the harvest. However, for Job the principal association of the dunghill is with the body. It is this latter connection that Mankind reflects in his speech:

> O thou my soull, so sotyll in thy substance,
> Alasse, what was thi fortune and thi chaunce
>   To be assocyat wyth my flesch, that stynkyng dungehyll?
> (ll. 202-04)

It may be useful to make reference to a continental altarpiece of c.1480-83--i.e., an item almost contemporary with the play *Mankind*--which illustrates Job seated in the left foreground upon the dunghill. He is nude, and he has his garment flung beside him. Though he is being afflicted with boils by a gruesome devil who stands behind his right shoulder, he nevertheless has his hands joined in prayer, and his eyes stare unfocused into space in indifference to his uncomfortable condition. His patience is in obvious contrast to the figure of the man attempting to pull a thorn from his foot in the sculpture at Wells Cathedral. Job's vision is not turned in upon his own discomfort or selfishly upon his own pain, but rather he is unconcerned with the things of this world.[57] Thus Job will not even notice the ugliness of the devil, or of the three additional demonic figures (Job's three friends unmasked, we may wonder?) in this altarpiece. Mankind, when confronted by the afflictions of his enemies, will not be able thus to persevere.

Reference to the iconography of Job *in stercore* will also assist in the interpretation of yet another aspect of the play, the scatological language that is so pervasive in the drama. Until recently, this language had seemed to most critics and many editors of the play to be excessively crude and offensive; Joseph Quincy Adams hence refused to print the most "vulgar" words and passages in his edition of the play in *Chief Pre-Shakespearean Dramas* (1924), a book which remained the principal textbook of medieval drama in introductory graduate courses in the United States until the appearance of David Bevington's *Medieval Drama* (1975). But if the author of *Mankind* were indeed drawing upon the symbolism of the dunghill in the story of Job, the scatological images would be precisely appropriate. A primary association of the devil is with dirt and excrement, the opposite of food and symbolic of decay. In a panel of early fifteenth-century painted glass in the Church of St. Michael, Spurriergate, York, the fallen Lucifer is shown with his formerly glorious feathers now bedraggled and dirty as he begins the transformation to an ugly, hairy demon (fig. 7). Beside him are two other fallen angels which have already been changed into the ugliest of creatures.[58] The York play of the *Creation of Heaven and Earth*, for example, also strongly emphasizes the change; even the devils' food now "es but filth" (Play I, l. 106). In painted glass in the West Window at Fairford, a devil appears with a mouth shaped like an anus (fig. 6). Additionally, the wit with which the scatological material is presented in *Mankind* brings the members of the audience into the action of the play as participants--and hence as sharing in the guilt. Such is the case especially in the bawdy "Crystemes songe" which New-Guise, Nowadays, and Nought teach to those sitting at the play (ll. 335-43)--a song which Paula Neuss has suggested is linked to the discordant music produced by Job's friends.[59] The music of this song must have been intended to seem very unlike the harmony of Creation.

The testing of Mankind also breaks down in part over his need to look after the demands of his body, particularly the bodily urge to defecate which takes him temporarily away from the task of sowing at a crucial time. We have noticed that he had identified his "flesch" with the stench of a "dungehyll" earlier in the play (l. 204)--an attempt to deny his body within the context of his early asceticism, which is now about to collapse. At lines 561-63, he excuses himself in response to Titivillus' suggestion that "Nature compellys":

I wyll into thi yerde, souerens, and cum ageyn son.
For drede of the colyke and eke of the ston

MANKIND

I wyll go do that nedys must be don.

He puts aside his prayer beads ("My bedys xall be here for whosummeuer wyll ellys," l. 564), and leaves the acting area to relieve himself of bodily waste in both kinds. Again the association with Job helps to serve to contrast Mankind with the Old Testament figure, who was regarded in the late Middle Ages as a man who prefigured Christ specifically in his suffering during the Passion.[60]

The character who engineers Mankind's collapse in the play is thus the devil Titivillus, who has been brought on stage by Mischief and his three cohorts following the collection of money from the audience. Both the *quête*, which is directly associated with the folk drama,[61] and the appearance of the devil on stage are immensely effective from a theatrical standpoint. Titivillus' entry is the most spectacular point in the drama, though to Mankind he will be invisible. Described as "the Fend of helle" (l. 886), he extends the malice of Mischief and his friends, who are now intent on revenge for the beating Mankind has given them, and thus he exemplifies the collaboration between the forces of the World and of the Devil.

In traditional iconography, Titivillus (or, more commonly, *Tutivillus*) is the demon normally assigned to collect words misspoken or mumbled at Mass and other services. He is described in *Jacob's Well*, which has been regarded as a possible source for *Mankind*:

> Jacobus de vitriaco tellyth that an holy man stood in cherch in a qwere, and seyg a feend beryng a gret sacchell full of thyng. The feend, as the man askyd the feend what he bare, the feend seyde: "I bere in my sacche sylablys and woordys, ouerskyppyd and synkopyd, and verse and psalmys the whiche these clerkys han stolyn in the qweere, and haue fayled in here seruyse."[62]

He is familiar to students of the drama through his appearance in the Towneley Judgment Play, where he is said to be a "courte rollar." His self-introduction in that play is very revealing:

> Mi name is tutiuillus,

> my horne is blawen;
> ffragmina verborum /
>   tutiuillus colligit horum,
> Belzabub algorum /
>   belial belium doliorum.[63]

From the literary evidence, Titivillus emerges as a demon who is both a threat to human beings and a comic figure; hence he is entirely appropriate to the play of *Mankind*.[64] He is assigned to look after the slothful in the saying of devotions, and for this purpose, as the passage from *Jacob's Well* indicates, he is given a sack to collect all idly misspoken and missed words in the service. But first he must record such words--a task he does by writing them down on a scroll. It is at this task that we normally see him in the visual arts, as on a bench end at Charlton Mackrell (fig. 8) and on a misericord in Ely Cathedral.[65] The latter shows a devil appearing between two women, one of whom has a rosary and the other a book; obviously he is eavesdropping upon their idle conversation in church. On the supporters of the misericord are two small devils, each with a scroll. The comic side of Titivillus' task is emphasized in Robert of Brunne's *Handlyng Synne*,[66] where the story is told of the demon who runs out of space to write down the words: he pulls at the roll with his teeth, and the parchment breaks, with the result that his head thumps loudly against a wall. The sound and sight of the devil hitting his head appropriately inspire laughter.[67]

    The Titivillus of *Mankind* has all the exaggerated traits of the devil who is at once the butt of laughter and yet a creature to be feared: he is comic, and yet he is indicative of evil forces which must be respected in spite of his absurdity. He thunders that he is the lord of lords--a regal dignity--and yet almost instantly begs "ser New Gys" for the loan of "a peny" (ll. 475, 478). When Nought, New-Guise, and Nowadays leave the stage, he gives them his curse: "Goo yowr wey, a deull wey, go yowr wey all!/ I blysse you wyth my lyfte honde: foull yow befall!" (ll. 521-22). Needless to say, the left-hand blessing is indicative of the malice of the underworld of darkness from which Titivillus comes: it is the reverse blessing of witches and wizards, whose hatred of wisdom and light also leads them to perform their rites at midnight in deepest darkness.[68]

Nowhere, to my knowledge, does Titivillus appear with a net in traditional iconography, though the use of a net would seem in the play Mankind to be entirely appropriate. "Euer I go invysybull, yt ys my jett," Titivillus announces, "Ande befor hys ey thus I wyll hange my nett/ To blench hys syght" (ll. 529-31). In *Job*, for example, Baldad says, "For he hath thrust his feet into a net, and walketh in its meshes. . . . A gin [*KJ:* snare] is hidden for him in the earth, and his trap upon the path" (18.8, 10). Frequently the psalms also call attention to nets and other means of entrapment (e.g., Psalm 9.16) which the spiritually wary would attempt by all means to avoid. In *Mankind*, however, the protagonist is unable to escape the effects of the net, which, according to the devil Titivillus, will "blench" or deceive his eyesight (l. 531).

Titivillus is in fact a trickster whose "game" (l. 605) provides a key to the iconographic context of the play. First, as we have seen, this antagonist of the process of sowing hides a board "wnder the erth preuely" (l. 533), and then he promises to "menge hys corne wyth drawke and wyth durnell;/ Yt xall not be lyke to sow nor to sell" (ll. 537-38). The purpose of the first is to force him to "lose hys pacyens" (l. 536), a virtue which, as we have seen, was traditionally associated with the figure of Job from the Old Testament. The second promise is consistent with another parable of the Sower and the Seed in St. Matthew's Gospel: "But while men were asleep, his enemy came and oversowed cockle [*L:* zizania; *KJ:* tares] among the wheat and went his way" (*Matt.* 13.25). Lorraine Stock has shown that *zizania* is the Latin equivalent of 'drawke' and 'durnell,' and she also cites medieval opinion that the sower's reaction to his enemy's subversive sowing is indicative of the virtue of patience.[69] But Mankind hardly reacts with patience when he attempts to dig in the ground and hits Titivillus' board, or when his bag of seed, his spade, and his prayer beads are stolen.[70] Instead, he becomes angry and all too easily is defeated in his task. "Of labure and preyer," he says, "I am nere yrke of both" (l. 585). Paradoxically, Mankind, instead of doing as Mercy would have him do, now will insist on falling asleep: "I xall slepe full my bely and he wore my brother" (l. 588). Such a sleep is indicative of a fall into the sin of Sloth, which in this context should be seen as particularly dangerous to the well-being of the soul.

The ability of Titivillus to deceive through direct suggestion that will enter a person's thoughts is within the usual powers of the medieval devil, who may thereby go undetected by the unwary. At first, Titivillus only convinces Mankind that he should set aside his appointed task of prayer in order to look after his bodily functions, but when he sleeps the devil plays a more elaborate trick upon him in order to entrap him: "A praty game xall be scheude yow or ye go hens" (l. 591). The trick involves a libel. Mercy, the devil says, has stolen a mare and has fled the country, and rumor has it that he has died in France, either by falling from his horse or by hanging. Trust Mercy no more, the devil advises, but instead "Aryse and aske mercy of Neu Gyse, Nowadays, and Nought" (l. 602). Finally, in words that in part foreshadow Mephostophilis' to Doctor Faustus,[71] Titivillus suggests that Mankind should deceive his wife and take a mistress.

The process by which Mankind turns away from the work of sowing and succumbs to temptation is described by Siegfried Wenzel in terms of the medieval understanding of the sin of Sloth, which has been noted above as characterizing this character's condition after his meeting with Titivillus. Wenzel comments: "Mankind falls through tedium in doing good works, which is caused by the bodily hardship that accompanies good works, both physical and spiritual. He gives in to sleep and thus becomes fully a prey to the devil, who then leads him to all sorts of sins and to Mischief."[72] Mankind becomes more and more weary as he approaches full-scale rebellion, and the lethargy that he feels is a usual sign of Sloth. He becomes more and more negligent of his religious duties, failing to go to church for evensong and instead kneeling to say his prayers in the field--prayers which, though brief (he is saying the *Pater Noster*, typically regarded as a usefully short prayer), are nevertheless broken off. "Do wey!" he says, "I wyll no more oft ouer the chyrche-style" (l. 583). When John Mirk comments on the sin of Sloth in his Septuagesima sermon in his *Festial*, he speaks of it as a sin which keeps one away from "Goddys seruyce liyng yn the morrowtyde long in bedde for owtrage wakyng ouer nyght."[73] Inevitably, Mankind must go to sleep, since his head is "very heuy" (l. 587). The bed or normal place of sleeping is, indeed, a common emblem of Sloth. In the representation of the Seven Deadly Sins formerly in the wall painting at Ingatestone, Essex, Sloth is the figure at the bottom of the wheel--a man in bed.[74]

Sloth is also indicated in the play by the language utilized in the temptation scene. As Wenzel points out, the word "wnlusty" in the line "Thys londe ys so harde yt makyth wnlusty and yrke" (l. 545) precisely indicates the Sloth which is behind Mankind's lethargy, and also "yrke" has an association with the same sin.[75] The resulting unhappy spiritual condition points in the direction of Mankind's despair later in the play--a despair that is aggravated by his belief that Mercy has permanently left him.

To establish better the context of sleep-sloth-despair versus mercy-hope, it seems useful to refer to a parable that does not appear directly in the play, though the principles established in this parable were broadly influential in the Middle Ages. The parable is that of the Wise and Foolish Virgins in St. Matthew's Gospel (25.1-13). The five foolish virgins in the parable fail to provide oil for their lamps--i.e., they fail to remain vigilant--and hence they have the door closed upon them when the Bridegroom arrives unexpectedly. As the early medieval music-drama from St. Martial of Limoges which had dramatized this parable shows, the spiritual lethargy that overcomes the foolish virgins will in the end bring them to a most unpleasant fate.[76] Émile Mâle notes that the high Middle Ages placed the foolish virgins on the left of Christ in the visual arts, and the wise virgins appeared on his right--exactly the orientation that will appear in the depictions of the Last Judgment that were to become so popular in English wall paintings.[77] In the late Middle Ages, the continental artist Martin Schongauer illustrated the ten figures of the parable, with the foolish virgins being shown as extremely well dressed ladies who, in their despair, hold their lamps downward to signify their emptiness, allow their hair to fall down carelessly, and weep tears which signify their hopeless state. At the end of history, the foolish will be those who have allowed their thoughts of pleasure to extinguish all their devotion. In contrast, the wise are vividly aflame with holy love which motivates their vigilance even unto the end.[78] A convenient English example illustrating the Wise and Foolish Virgins is the painted glass at Melbury Bubb, Dorset (fig. 10).

Upon awakening from his lethargic and slothful sleep, Mankind hastens toward the "ale-house" to "speke wyth New Gyse, Nowadays and Nought/ And geett me a lemman wyth a smattrynge face" (ll. 609-11). The tavern would be an appropriate place for him to retreat to at this time; it is the location to which, for example, Mary Magdalene is taken on her descent from virtue in the Digby play.[79] It is also the place where Mankind will soon promise to spend Sunday mornings "And forbere masse and matens, owres and prime" (ll. 711-12). As medieval writers commonly asserted, the tavern is the devil's church where the Seven Deadly Sins are taught and practiced.[80] At this point in the play, before Mankind can get away, New-Guise and the other scoundrels arrive in the playing area.

All the Vices come on stage here with evidence of criminal behavior except Nought, who is angered that he has not been able to steal. New-Guise, still wearing the noose that was around his neck when the rope "brast asonder" at his hanging (l. 616), had been condemned by a court of law for stealing a horse. He appears as the archetypal desperate man with the emblem of his inner condition about his neck. Mischief, who had been able to recite his neck verse, has been sentenced to prison, but has broken jail. The fetters which he wears are indicative of very great shame. Paula Neuss has suggested[81] that his recitation of the neck verse is itself highly ironic in the light of the context of the opening of Psalm 50 (51), which provided the test of a person's Latin and hence of his clerical status:

> Have mercy upon me, O God, according to thy great mercy. And according to the multitude of thy tender mercies blot out my iniquity....

At the ultimate level of impudence and criminality, Nowadays has come into the acting area with the fruits of his thievery, which include church plate and the Sacrament. To this rowdy crew, then, Mankind addresses his absurd plea for forgiveness: "I crye yow mercy of all that I dyde amysse" (l. 658)! As we might expect when an individual pledges himself to the lower powers, the state of things has iconographically been turned upside down. Mankind, who has utterly forgotten the task of sowing which had been laid upon him, now will have his name written in Mischief's book, which may be identified as precisely opposed to the Book of Life designated in the *Apocalypse*.[82]

But having Mankind's name enrolled in Mischief's book is too important a matter to be done without a regular court sessions, which is duly proclaimed by Nowadays. Nought is steward, though as a fool he knows no Latin--a lack that causes him to muddle the legal documents that he writes, even giving the regnal year of King Edward as "nothing" ("Anno regni regitalis/ Edwardi nullateni") (ll. 689-90). New-Guise then helps Mankind to outfit himself in clothing more suited to his new life of vice; taking away his quite proper long gown, he brings it back much shortened--and then takes it out once more to return it at last transformed into a very short (and ridiculous) "jakett" (l. 718). In addition to legal prohibitions against short gowns "unless it be of such length that the same may cover his privy members and buttocks,"[83] such a short jacket would be particularly inappropriate for one appearing in a court of law. He is indeed made to appear like a fool, who may, as we have seen in the instance of the illustration of the fool in the Barlow Psalter, appear dressed only in a hood--i.e., in a garment which is not sufficient to provide decent cover for the body. However, since the court of Mischief reverses exactly the order of things, Mankind's indecent clothing reflects the lack of decorum to be expected before such a lord.

It has been noted by Neuss[84] that the manorial court of Mischief provides a parody of the Last Judgment as it was presented in the English civic cycles. Instead of the Corporal Acts of Mercy, the Deadly Sins of Lechery, Infidelity, and Wrath are solemnly proclaimed, while Mankind in each instance gives his assent to them. The mock court, however, breaks up at the appearance of Mercy, and all the participants go off to play a game of football, a very rough game that was regarded as an illegal sport.[85] Since Mercy is now left alone on stage, he is here able to lament what has happened to transform Mankind, who has ungratefully

MANKIND

broken his most solemn promises and has ruined himself: "To God and to all the holy corte of hewyn thou [i.e., Mankind] art despectyble" (l. 752). Mankind's defection is particularly lamentable, since God's own Son had shed his blood entirely to purify Mankind's "iniquite" (l. 745). Because he fears so deeply for Mankind's end, Mercy prays to the Virgin Mary, weeps bitter tears, and actively sets out to search for him.

The final portion of the play focuses on the judgment of God--the process by which the chaff will be separated from the wheat--which Mankind, having been shocked out of his lethargy, now comes to expect and even to desire as his just ending. In his despair he seeks suicide, which, as noted above, is the ending assigned to the fool or his companion in certain psalter illustrations. "A roppe, a rope, a rope!" Mankind cries, "I am not worthy" (l. 800). Mischief already has the rope ready for him, and it is attached to a gallows. New-Guise demonstrates the noose, putting it about his own neck:

> Lo, Mankynde! do as I do; this ys thi new gyse.
> Gyff the roppe just to thy neke; this ys myn avyse.
>
> (ll. 804-05)

New-Guise's comic accident in almost hanging himself does not lessen the seriousness of the predicament that Mankind is in, and the presence of the gallows on the stage presents for the audience a sign that designates his spiritual condition. The earliest extant example of the Crucifixion in the visual arts, an ivory of c.410 A.D., is useful in representing an aspect of traditional iconography that would remain constant through the Middle Ages; in this instance, the death of Christ on the cross is set over against the death by hanging of Judas on the other side: hope through the sacrifice of Christ is contrasted to the ultimate illustration of despair, which logically and inevitably led to the suicide of the former apostle.[86] In depictions of despair during the late Middle Ages, suicide is a common result of the loss of all hope by an individual. Thus, as we have seen, the king who appears with the fool in certain psalters[87] will stab himself to death with his own sword. If, as Psalms 13 (14) and 52 (53) indicate, the fool says that there is no

God, then the person who believes the fool's words will condemn himself to an unhappy ending. It is also no accident that Despaire in Spenser's *Faerie Queene* will be a tempter who tries to coerce the Red Crosse Knight into choosing one means or another for a self-inflicted death.[88]

However, Mankind, instead of hanging himself, falls before Mercy in a posture of humiliation. His despair is still real, and it is graphically illustrated through the position of his body. But it is also the posture of supplication, and hence his despair will in the end also point him toward hope rather than death and eternal punishment. This is so because despair can be of two kinds, one ending in death as Judas ended and the other in life and renewal.[89] The first kind of despair is typically illustrated by an influential continental example, the figure in Giotto's famous fresco in the Arena Chapel at Padua where the despairing woman is hanging herself--an act to which she is prompted by a demon.[90] On the other hand, the second kind of despair may be illustrated by the case of St. Augustine, to whom despair ultimately was a prelude to renewal.[91] So too will it be in the case of Mankind, who will be able to rise again to his feet in a symbolic action that will reflect his inner state. In spite of his protests to the contrary, he will through the power of God's mercy "be rewyvyd and restoryd ageyn" (l. 832), for God does not desire the death of a sinner ("Nolo mortem peccatoris, inquit," l. 834). Within the action of the play, Mercy shall ask Mankind to rise from his fallen condition.

The conclusion of *Mankind* thus turns on the protagonist's penitential experience of being "rewyvyd and restoryd ageyn"--terms that seem suspiciously like gardening terms--with Mercy mediating between the sinner and the deity. Though Mankind's confession is freely handled, its iconography nevertheless depends on the sacrament of penance as frequently illustrated in the visual arts. Mischief's frightened words--"Lo, Mercy ys here!/ He skaryth ws wyth a bales" (ll. 806-07)--indicate that Mercy carries a scourge or rod. The rod appears, for example, in British Library Add. MS. 25,698, fol. 9: this miniature from the fifteenth century shows the priest, who is giving absolution to a man kneeling before him, touching the penitent lightly upon the head with the rod.[92] In

MANKIND

early fourteenth-century glass in the nave of York Minster, scenes in the Penancers Window illustrate the presence of the scourge rather than the rod. In *Mankind*, Mercy in his priestly role appears before the penitent, who would appropriately kneel, as in the extant illustrations from the late Middle Ages, without the privacy of an enclosed confessional. And, after warning Mankind about the dangers of the World, the Flesh, and the Devil, Mercy allows him to go on his way: "Take your lewe whan ye wyll. God send yow good perseuerans!" (l. 898). Thereupon Mankind says:

> Syth I schall departe, blyse me, fader, her then I go.
> God send ws all plente of hys gret mercy!
> (ll. 899-900)

Finally, Mercy pronounces a blessing upon Mankind:

> Dominus custodit te ab omni malo
> In nomine Patris et Filii et Spiritus Sancti.
> Amen! (ll. 901-02)

The end of the play is not an ending but a beginning, for now Mankind will again be sent forth into the world to serve with gladness of heart. In the epilogue, Mercy urges this kind of service upon the members of the audience sitting or standing at the play; they are asked to think about Christ's humanity and their own "condicyons" (l. 908). Through Mankind's experience, the audience may also have come to understand its spiritual state and to recognize that life requires to be lived with the end of life in mind. ("Be repentant here, trust not the owr of deth; thynke on this lessun:/ 'Ecce nunc tempus acceptabile, ecce nunc dies salutis'," Mercy had told Mankind [ll. 865-66].) Appropriately, the play concludes with a blessing upon the audience "That ye may be pleyferys wyth the angellys abowe/ And hawe to your porcyon vitam eternam. Amen" (ll. 913-14).

In spite of all the difficulties of living one's life, the play's optimistic conclusion is that sowing can still be fruitful and that despair need not be the inevitable affliction attendant on the life of a man or woman. The iconography which provides the essential context for the play is hence not simple but rather is quite complicated; also this iconography is, to be sure, not totally consistent, for the protagonist is at once the sower and the one whose heart is the recipient of the seed of faith and salvation. In the action of the play as in life as perceived in the late fifteenth century, causes can be detached from their normally inevitable effects by means of the mercy of God. Indeed, the conclusion of the play suggests that, in spite of man's lapsarian condition, the harvest for him may even be one of joy and everlasting life.

II

THE CASTLE OF PERSEVERANCE: THE ICONOGRAPHY OF ALIENATION AND RECONCILIATION

A study of *The Castle of Perseverance* by Milla Riggio has usefully established the social and political background against which this drama requires to be seen. While the play is clearly a protest against the demands placed upon the individual by the world, particularly as these demands were expressed in East Anglia where political and social control was maintained by the great magnates of the region, no modern solution (e.g., reform or revolution) is proposed. As Riggio suggests, "Instead of reflecting a desire for social reform this critique of society [by the playwright] provides a formal vehicle for the conservative Christian ideal of *contemptus mundi*."[1] The play, then, especially stresses the alienation from God and from the ideal life of religious devotion and virtue that occurs when one submits himself (or herself) to the social and political pressures of the time.

The solution proffered to mankind in *The Castle of Perseverance* is the reconciliation that is possible for members of the race through the life of devotion, through the Sacraments, and through good works. Humanum Genus, the protagonist, will experience both success and (more extensively) failure in his pursuit of this kind of life, and in the end the scene of the Four Daughters of God will provide the culminating illustration of reconciliation that will establish the basis for his final victory over the forces of darkness. But, in spite of the conclusion of the play which offers grace to a seemingly undeserving person (except for his final declaration), the drama's conflict and attendant tensions derive finally from a binary view of things in which the individual is expected to align himself or herself with the heavenward orientation of existence and to reject the lower orders of existence that are represented by the Three Enemies of Man--i.e., the World, the Flesh, and the Devil--who ring a person around in this life.

Such an understanding of the human predicament is reflected in the staging plan for *The Castle of Perseverance* that appears on fol. 191ᵛ of the manuscript (fig. 9). This plan, to which we shall return below for further discussion of its implications for the play, places the castle, or place of safety, in the center--a zone of safety where the properly oriented individual may be secure from the assaults of the World, the Flesh, and the Devil and the attendant Vices--while at one side is located the scaffold of God that represents the direction to which one needs to look if one is to escape the threatening figures on the other scaffolds encircling the playing area or platea. And the location of God's scaffold is in the East. Hence the proper movement of the protagonist in the play should be toward the East, toward God, who remains throughout a focus of hope for Humanum Genus.[2] This movement may be represented as schematically indicated on the next page. The layout of the stage is here not unrelated to that of a church, which in England would normally face toward the East, the direction established in medieval thought as that of the Second Coming of Christ. The chancel is hence in the east end of the church, and the people ordinarily face in that direction, which further defines the direction of the Christian journey toward the salvation symbolized by the heavenly Jerusalem. Eastward movement in this life was regarded as the direction of the individual Christian when he or she crosses under the chancel arch to receive Communion, the Eucharistic bread that participates, according to medieval theology, in the deepest mysteries of salvation history and further provides a foretaste of the great wedding feast awaiting men and women beyond the Judgment Day. It is no accident, therefore, that wall paintings of the Last Judgment were frequently placed over the chancel arch of the church as symbolic reminders to the parishioners of the true direction and ending point of their lives.[3] So too will the members of the audience of *The Castle of Perseverance*, like its protagonist, be warned to "thynke on thyn endynge day" (l. 407) when the next moment of consciousness will be awakening to the Last Judgment. This intended audience response is implied generally in the morality genre, though, as the final chapter of this study will emphasize, the iconography of death and dying is not always made part of the literal stage picture included in the play. In the drama under consideration in this chapter, however, Death will not only be present literally, but also will be personified in the manner which we associate with the Dance of Death motif—a motif that will receive full treatment in Chapter IV, below. Through the vision of the future provided by the drama, the audience is able to visualize its own fate and to foresee the rituals of death that are common to all men and women, who thus are reminded of their mortality.

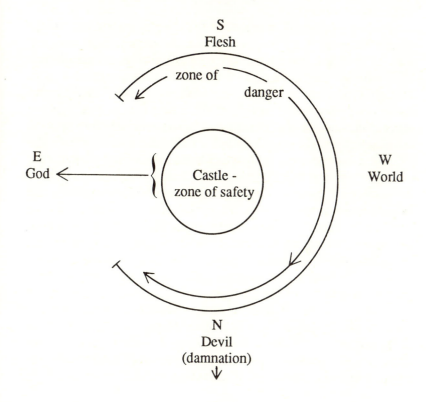

Nevertheless, *The Castle of Perseverance* is not liturgy, and its setting is not a church but rather a space that is only analogous to the architecture of the church building. As drama, it is play which instead introduces the element of the imagination to create an action that illustrates the expected tension between the demands of religion and the alienation from the religious life likely to take place in the world. The introduction of the imaginative element does not, however, mean that the iconography of the play will be innovative or, in modern terms, "original." Rather, the theme of alienation vs. reconciliation which runs through the entire play quite naturally finds expression in such traditional iconography as that of the Ages of Man, the battle of the Virtues and Vices, the coming of Death as in the Dance of Death, and the reconciliation of the Four Daughters of God. Even the castle, which gives its name to the play, is not innovative but rather conventional in its origin, as we shall see.

But the playwright responsible for the play had in any case a clear sense of the theatrical, and, while the banns suggest performance on the town green, the drama's stage plan seems appropriate for a type of staging that was usual in the region of East Anglia. Though symbolic, the stage plan with its scaffolds and central castle fits perfectly the design of the East Anglian theater as we today understand it. As Richard Beadle has convincingly argued in his dissertation, the usual staging in East Anglia involved not the pageant wagon staging with which we have become so familiar, but rather place-and-scaffold staging.[4] Further, the round design of the stage plan for *The Castle of Perseverance* corresponds to the general shape of the outdoor theaters of East Anglia as these have been conjecturally reconstructed. For example, the "game place" or theater located at Walsham-le-Willows, Suffolk, was in fact described in the sixteenth century as "a place compassed rownd with a fayer banke cast vp on a good height and havinge many great trees called populers growynge about the same banke, in the myddest a fayre round place of earth wythe a stone wall about the same to the height of the earth made of purpose for the vse of Stage playes. . . ."[5] Such theatrical space, which seems to have been round, possibly was modeled on the ancient Roman amphitheaters.[6] However, it also may reflect either the lists, sometimes round in shape, used in tournaments or the rounds found elsewhere in England--e.g., the round near Penrith, Cumbria, which was known as "King Arthur's Round Table." This very large round contained a ditch and embankment which surrounded a *platea* that would have been suitable for staging plays.[7] The documentation of such theaters in England in the late Middle Ages provides support for understanding *The Castle of Perseverance* as a play designed for presentation--and, as the production which was mounted at the University of Toronto has proven,[8] the play is one that is remarkably effective when presented before an audience.

The alienation and tensions resulting from the inherited condition of mankind are immediately made visible from the beginning of the first scene when this play is presented in the theater. The new-born Humanum Genus appears in the *platea*, where he walks about in clockwise fashion and addresses the various scaffolds in turn.[9] His human vulnerability is underlined, and he is made very aware of the two angels--one good and one filled with malice--assigned to him. His movement, circling about the *platea*, does not, however, suggest a direction that will lead immediately to salvation--i.e., it neither leads directly to the East where God has his scaffold, nor does it necessarily imply a pilgrimage that would ultimately take the protagonist to the heavenly kingdom. Hence Humanum Genus is not actually to be seen as setting out in any clear sense on a pilgrimage, which would involve the earnest and deliberate movement of a man or woman, separated from home and country and encountering liminal experience, toward a much desired transcendental goal.[10] Yet in the medieval view shared by the author of *The Castle of Perseverance*, all men and women are to some extent properly strangers and wayfarers in this world, and to a degree the condition implied by the idea of man-as-wanderer is of necessity to be regarded as shared by Humanum Genus at this point. Such a condition is opposed, for example, to that of New-Guise and Nowadays in *Mankind* who represent being totally at home in this world and hence being blind to the realities of existence.[11]

For Humanum Genus, the conflict is initially between conformity and a state of grace, between indulgence in the Seven Deadly Sins and the rejection of their influence. Though his spiritual desire is too weak to lead him on a fully developed pilgrimage, he is nevertheless able to muddle through and to achieve in the end the reward granted to those who participate on the side of mercy in the skirmishes which take place in this world. As Siegfried Wenzel points out, *The Castle of Perseverance* lacks a "questing hero" of the type that would be required in a true pilgrimage play,[12] which would have been expected to take note of the traditions of pilgrimage as practiced in an age when such journeying was highly significant as an accepted form of religious experience.[13] The stage design, utilizing the form of a circle rather than a linear path such as would have been marked by a processional drama on pageant wagons, further argues against seeing the play in terms of pilgrimage: instead, the action folds back around itself, achieving not a unity in any formal sense but rather a dramatic structure that suggests the vicissitudes of human life as it is lived between the polarities of evil and good in this world.

The shape of the stage, then, is the basis for one level of iconography in the play. In the current debate over the staging of the drama, the controversial stage plan of Richard Southern as presented in his *Medieval Theatre in the Round*[14] fails to take into account the manner in which the diagram in the Macro manuscript schematizes the moral order which confronts mankind. We have already noted that the diagram in the manuscript illustrates how Humanum Genus is trapped on three sides and how his escape must be only through movement toward the East, the direction traditionally associated with hope and life just as West is associated with despair and death. In a diagram which places, for example, the scaffold of the devil at once to the north and at the bottom of the drawing because these are the directions that are iconographically correct,[15] the ditch around the castle also must serve an iconographic rather than merely practical purpose.[16] Logically, this ditch, filled with the "watyr of grace" (l. 2329), should circumscribe not the entire area that Humanum Genus will "walke" and "wende" between his birth and death, but rather only the area where he will seek protection from the World, the Flesh, and the Devil as well as from the Vices who are associated with them.

The movement from birth to death in the play is indicative

further of man's condition as inheriting the pattern of creation, fall, recovery, and ultimately death and return to dust of the first member of the race. Humanum Genus' first lines in the play thus refer to forms and shapes as they affect man at his birth:

> Aftyr oure forme-faderys kende
> This nyth I was of my modyr born.
> (ll. 275-76)

As a new-born child, he has taken his form from his primordial ancestor, Adam, who founded the race at the beginning of time. Having come naked into this world, he has been "schapyn and schorn" by his heredity, and now is covered only by his baptismal garment. Ultimately he has been derived through Adam from the earth itself, "And as erthe I stande this sele" (l. 298). And at the end of his life he will return again to earth--a returning that, as we have seen in the previous chapter, the liturgy proclaims in the rites for Ash Wednesday. Through this life, then, from birth to death, Humanum Genus will experience within himself the drama of the dialectic of rising and falling, of hope and false hope and despair, and in the end a remarkable instance of salvation that, through the grace which is symbolically present in the play, extends beyond what he seems to deserve to lift him up into bliss at the last.

The organization of the stages along life's way in *The Castle of Perseverance* is dependent on the traditional iconography of the Seven Ages of Man,[17] which defines the temporal segments of his earthly existence in terms of lesser and greater degrees of devotion to the religious ideals and of alienation from those ideals. To be sure, this iconography is occasionally somewhat blurred in the play, but a number of points in Humanum Genus' life are very clearly defined, while the remaining periods are nevertheless implied by the text. As we have seen, the protagonist has his beginning as a newly born child in his nakedness who is baptised and who then grows toward adulthood. "A crysyme I haue and no moo," he comments near the end of his first long speech (l. 324). By line 396, when Humanum Genus indicates that he wishes to "go play" with the World, he has clearly passed over into the second stage of his life--a stage that is comparable to the second period as defined in "Of the Seven Ages," a rhymed dialogue of the early fifteenth century with marginal illustrations (fig. 11) that appears in British Library MS. Add. 37,049, fols. 28v-29r.[18] This poetic dialogue, which offers a most useful analogue to *The Castle of Perseverance* and very clearly sets forth each of the Seven Ages of Man according to the traditional iconography, provides an excellent parallel to the child in the play; "I wil go play with my felowe," the child in this poem insists.[19]

Thereafter, the period of Humanum Genus' youth is defined as unruly, as in the case of the protagonist in "Of the Seven Ages," by his rising interest in the opposite sex and in various of the Seven Deadly Sins. If we may believe Malus Angelus in the play, by line 1575 he has passed through mature manhood and has arrived at forty years of age, considered then to be the beginning of old age;[20] only because he is extremely fortunate will his strength now even at first remain stable prior to declining as his years increase. It is in this period of post-maturity that Humanum Genus is brought to the castle, a location that signifies a rejection of the Sins and of the Three Enemies of Man. Here he seems yet at the highest point of his spiritual strength. However, all too soon his strength will begin to decline along with his ability to resist evil. In spite of the successful repulsing of the various Deadly Sins by the Virtues, Covetousness will in the end reclaim him for a life that is separated from the spiritual alignment which the castle represents. He has become vulnerable to the sin of Covetousness that most often afflicts older men who feel their strength slipping away:

> I gynne to waxyn hory and olde.
> My bake gynnyth to bowe and bende,
> I crulle and crepe and wax al colde.
> Age makyth man ful vnthende,
> Body and bonys and al vnwolde;
> My bonys are febyl and sore.
> (ll. 2482-87)

Alienated because of his age, his appearance and clothing are now changed, and at this point in his life he wears "a sloppe" (l. 2488), an appropriate gown for an old man. His hair is all gray, while he also complains that his "nose is colde and gynnyth to droppe" (l. 2490). Such a figure is illustrated in the marginal illustration in "Of the Seven Ages"[21] where the man with prayer beads is being tempted by the bad angel at his left shoulder. In the play, Covetousness urges Humanum Genus to recognize the perils of old age, which he suggests is not a good period in one's life if one is poor. But, as Humanum Genus discovers, in the end Death will come to all men, rich or poor. Indeed, riches serve only as a hindrance to one's welfare and as a source of alienation, since at this point in his life he must at last face the inevitable fact of dying. Lying on his deathbed as in the illumination in "Of the Seven Ages," Humanum Genus will in the end deliver up his soul, which is illustrated as like a little child (fig. 11).[22]

In Longthorpe Tower, near Peterborough, a wall painting provides further illustration of the iconography of the Seven Ages of Man. The stages along life's way here are *Infans*, placed on the left and shown in a cradle; *Puer*, playing with a spinning top; *Adolescens* (very little remaining); *Vir*, as a hunter with a hawk on his wrist; *Adultus* (very little remaining); *Senectus*, holding a money bag; and *Decrepitus*, walking with crutches. These figures are shown rising in an arch to *Vir*, with decline beginning already with *Adultus*.[23] To be sure, this series does not at every point correspond to the sequence of the Seven Ages in *The Castle of Perseverance*, but there are nevertheless several details which are of considerable importance for our understanding of the play. For example, the association of avarice with old age involves iconography common to both wall painting and play, and we notice also the visualizing of a human life as a pattern of rising and falling strength. Yet the play suggests that man is most responsible and best able to defend himself against vice when he is in late adulthood--i.e., immediately as he begins the descent into one's final old age with its fearsome threat of poverty and ill health until at death he will be at last a passive figure poised between good and evil angels.[24]

The utilization of the good and evil angels in the play is, of course, critical to the binary moral and dramatic structure of *The Castle of Perseverance*. The good and evil angels are also at hand in the poetic dialogue "Of the Seven Ages," which visually shows their functioning in the accompanying illustrations (fig. 11). Even in early childhood, the grotesque bat-winged demon with its claws and horns will stand at the *left* or weaker side of the individual, while at his *right* will be placed the lovely figure of the good guardian angel wearing an alb and amice.[25] In each of the illustrations which show subsequent stages of the man's life in "Of the Seven Ages," these evil and good angels follow him, until at the end it is the good angel who rescues the soul of the individual lying on his deathbed. (The bad angel turns away, presumably in anger and envy.)[26] Conversely, in Marlowe's *Tragical History of Doctor Faustus*, the evil and tempting angel will be victorious over the protagonist in the play's last scene; with his cohorts, the bad angel in this play will seize on their victim with destructive glee. The possibility of such an unhappy ending is naturally present in *The Castle of Perseverance*. An example of such a failure to achieve salvation is present in an early tympanum now in the Yorkshire Museum; here in twelfth-century sculpture a demon clearly holds in his grasp the soul of a dying man.[27] Fear of such an end pervades the Middle Ages.

Both salvation and damnation are, of course, possible in the cosmos established by late medieval religion and reflected in *The Castle of Perseverance*. Life is presented as a series of binary moral decisions which ultimately will have the effect of determining one's everlasting state. As noted above, the one side, associated with evil and alienation, repeats the primordial fall of man in the Garden of Eden when Adam and Eve ate the forbidden fruit from the tree. But it also repeats an earlier fall--the fall of Lucifer from heaven as a result of his proud attempt to establish a position of primacy in the heavenly paradise. The latter explains, as we know, the origin of the fallen angels in the Judeo-Christian myths, and it is this kind of angel that provides one source for the iconographic tradition of the evil angel at the left side of the Christian. There is, however, another source in Greek thought: the presence of the personal spirit or daemon identified, for example, by Plato in the *Phaedo*[28]--a daemon that was interpreted very early in Christian thought as demonic or devilish. The Greek understanding of the daemon appears curiously to have influenced the idea of a guardian angel that had been present but not very well worked out in Jewish thinking.[29] New Testament support for the notion of the guardian angel is given in *Acts* 12.15, but as early as the second century the Shepherd of Hermas described the "two angels" which are "with man."[30] The "angel of righteousness" is thus set in contrast to the "angel of iniquity" who is "bitter, and angry, and foolish; and his works are pernicious, and overthrow the servants of God." The one speaks in one's heart of good works and righteousness, while the other speaks of pride, anger, ambition, and other sins.[31] In *The Castle of Perseverance*, Humanum Genus repeats the traditional theology and iconography:

> T[w]o aungels bene asynyd to me:
>   The ton techyth me to goode;
> On my ryth syde ye may hym se;
>   He cam fro Criste that deyed on rode.
> Anothyr is ordeynyd her to be
>   That is my foo, be fen and flode;
> He is about in euery degre
>   To drawe me to tho dewylys wode
>   That in helle ben thycke.
> Swyche t[w]o hath euery man on lyue
> To rewlyn hym and hys wyttys fyue.
> Whanne man doth ewyl, the ton wolde schryue,
>   The tothyr drawyth to wycke.
>   (ll. 301-13)

The one angel, therefore, comes "fro heuene trone" (l. 317) at birth to assist man or woman in walking the ways of the godly, while the other comes up from another place where hostile devils obtain satisfaction from the practice of torturing souls.

From the standpoint of the structure of the play, the two angels are of extreme significance, for at crucial times they initiate the action either toward good or toward evil, toward reconciliation and virtue or toward alienation and the Enemies of Man. Malus Angelus thus urges Humanum Genus toward the pleasures of the World, while Bonus Angelus insists that he should think about his "endynge day/ Whanne thou schalt be closyd vndyr clay" (ll. 407-08). The protagonist is told by one angel to wait until he is sixty years old before be repents in order that he might enjoy life in any way that may amuse him; the other warns him against such wilful folly which shall destroy him. "Ya, for this gamyn and this gle/ Thou schalt grocchyn and grone," Bonus Angelus explains (ll. 454-55). The guileful bad angel, however, is able to blind Humanum Genus and to lead him in the direction of the Seven Deadly Sins in spite of the irrationality of allowing himself to be thus entrapped by evil. And toward the good guardian angel, this demon is fully as hostile as we would expect him to be, accusing him of hypocrisy and inviting him to kiss his "nether ende" (ll. 813-14). But, in spite of the early success of the arrogant Malus Angelus, the good angel nevertheless is able to impell those forces into motion that will, at least temporarily, set Humanum Genus free from the wiles of the Three Enemies of Man and the Seven Deadly Sins. "I am abowte bothe day and nyth," he explains, "To brynge hys sowle into blis bryth" in spite of Humanum Genus' efforts to bring it "to pyne" (ll. 1270-72).

Paradoxically, Humanum Genus' *fall* into the snares of evil and alienation in *The Castle of Perseverance* involves the climbing of the protagonist *up* onto the scaffold of Covetousness, where he is joined by the other Deadly Sins and their companions. Thus to raise oneself up is to place oneself in a precarious position, for, as the Church Fathers insisted, by attempting to make himself more in this way, the ambitious sinner really makes himself less.[32] Humanum Genus therefore is placed quite appropriately upon a high and precarious seat--"on a stomlynge stol" (l. 1039)--from which he is expected to fall to the ground to his death. The high seat is, as Humanum Genus himself recognizes, identical with the highest position on Fortune's wheel, which is conveniently illustrated in the wall painting at Rochester Cathedral (fig. 12). The position at the top in the play is also described as the seat of the "seuene synnys" (l. 1315). Such an identification of a high seat with Fortune's wheel and the Seven Deadly Sins was also to be found in the wall painting formerly at Ingatestone, where Pride or Superbia, a fashionably dressed woman, was placed at the highest point of a Wheel of Fortune.[33]

The iconography of the Seven Deadly Sins in *The Castle of Perseverance* is traditional, though in order to fill out the complement of sins assigned to each of the Three Enemies of Man the author of the play adds two lesser sins, Lust-Liking (Voluptas) and Folly (Stultitia), who are assigned to the World in the first part of the play.[34] When Humanum Genus ascends to the scaffold of the World, therefore, these two will serve him, though with a sinister intent appropriate to these figures of alienation. Lust-liking will wrap him in rich clothing, while Folly will be his servant wherever he may go "Bothe nyth and day" (l. 630). As a typical fool, Folly clearly is to be associated with the iconography of the fool as discussed in the previous chapter of this study. However, as the Bible suggests, there may be two kinds of foolishness, and hence in this instance the foolishness that is depicted is of the type that cannot be perceived by one who is alienated from the divine perspective. If, therefore, reference may be made for the purpose of clarification to the delineation of these two types of foolishness in Shakespeare's *King Lear*, we will see that the foolishness is that of Goneril and Regan rather than of Cordelia.[35] The role of Lust-Liking is to assist in making Humanum Genus so comfortable in the world that he will forget to listen to his guardian angel or to judge events from any higher perspective than that provided by his Three Enemies and their followers. "Lete vs plesyn hym tyl that he rewe," Folly says, "In hell to hangyn hye" (ll. 723-24). Such is the danger of being set in the seat of the Seven Deadly Sins and at the top of Fortune's wheel.

Even in the first successful temptation of Humanum Genus, Covetousness has a principal role. Through Covetousness' seduction of him all the other Deadly Sins are able to enter. From the standpoint of the staging, this is quite appropriate, since Covetousness has a scaffold to himself at the northeast, between Belial in the north and God in the east. Covetousness is, after all, a less radical place to start one's life in sin than in direct company with the devil, and on the staging diagram the northeast scaffold is also the first one to which one would come when circling counterclockwise and to the left from an alignment with God's stage. This counterclockwise direction is not without significance, since we know that witches and other evil creatures also commonly tended to move in a counterclockwise fashion.[36] But the staging also suggests a reason for next calling out the lieutenants of the devil--i.e., Pride, Wrath, and Envy--for they are located nearby.

The others--Gluttony, Lechery, and Sloth--are not, however, far behind. Gluttony, as we would expect, offers release from fasting, while Lechery, who is a lovely woman in appearance, will go to bed with Humanum Genus and engage him in "fleschly folye" (l. 1185): "Therfore, Mankynd, my leue lemman,/ I my cunte thou schalt crepe" (ll. 1189-90). Sloth, as we would expect, will attempt to keep him in bed "Whanne the messe-belle goth" (l. 1212). Most commonly in iconography, as we have seen, Sloth is represented by a figure on or in a bed who is neglectful of his prayers.[37] Humanum Genus, now pleased with his new life of sin in spite of the dangerous implications of such an alienated existence for his eternal life, excuses himself because all men appear to be flawed: "I se no man but they vse somme/ Of these seuene dedly synnys" (ll. 1249-50). "Therfore," says Malus Angelus, "haue I now maystrye/ Welny ouyr al mankynde" (ll. 1284-85).

Bonus Angelus, however, sets forward the segment of the play's action which is now about to begin. The guardian angel's lament details the extent of Humanum Genus' fall and of the spiritual blindness caused by his alienated condition, and in one very important line he prays: "Mercy, God, that man were amendyd!" (l. 1297). "Mercy" is here as in Mankind an almost magic word, and the divine order indeed comes to the rescue of the play's protagonist who is so much in need of a change from one way of life to its opposite, from alienation to reconciliation. Two new personifications will come into the playing area--Shrift and Penance. Speaking to the first of these, the good angel laments further that Humanum Genus is deliberately avoiding him: "Wyth me he thynkyth neueremore to mete" (l. 1317). In a manner reminiscent of St. Basil's exegesis of Psalm 33, the state of sin exiles the guardian angel who should otherwise assist in providing protection against evil.[38] As we would expect, Humanum Genus will also have nothing to do with Shrift directly. Penance, however, is able to bring Humanum Genus to a radical change of attitude--the first step in the process of reconciliation which will bring him back into a state of grace.

Psychologically, Humanum Genus' conscience will be touched or "pricked." Penance's action at this point is presented in terms of an iconographic tableau that connects the effect on the man's conscience with the Christian myths that stand behind the psychology. He will reach up with his lance, which represents the "poynt of penaunce" (l. 1377), to thrust it into the core of Humanum Genus' heart. From the standpoint of formal artistic design, the scene is not so different from the familiar Crucifixion scene in which the blind Longinus reaches up with his spear to thrust it into Christ's side--an act which culminates in the soldier's miraculous gaining of his sight. Here, however, the meaning of the scene is precisely reversed, for the lance which causes the prick of conscience at Humanum Genus' heart is held by an allegorical figure that represents not a blind act but a deliberate intrusion of divine truth into the man's life. It is Humanum Genus, not the figure with the lance, who regains his sight, which will set the wounded man weeping with tears that are truly preparatory to reconciliation. Through the wound the well of mercy is opened up, and the sinful man is given the opportunity to participate in the Sacraments that will cleanse his soul. Nothing washes the soul more clean than "swete sorwe of hert," Penance insists (l. 1385). The immediate result will be that Humanum Genus will come down from the scaffold and will humble himself in a scene that is particularly effective from a theatrical point of view. His "sorwe of hert," caused by the prick of the lance, will be crucial in the process of arriving at the heavenly "bowre of blys" (ll. 1418-19).

The next stage in reconciliation will be the protagonist's confession, an act which possesses great cleansing power, as Shrift establishes. The scene, though didactic, is theatrically effective. Shrift carefully lessons Humanum Genus on the obligations of a person confessing his sins. He must acknowledge all his faults and not keep anything back if he wants to avoid having his soul sink "to Satanas/ In gastful glowynge glede" (ll. 1462-63).[39] Dutifully, Humanum Genus confesses that he has used the Seven Deadly Sins, has broken the Ten Commandments, and has misused his Five Wits; then he kneels, taking the traditional posture for absolution--a posture familiar to us from medieval manuscript illuminations.[40] Shrift will grant him absolution, and will advise him to sin no more so that he might protect himself from the state of alienation that he previously had experienced.

It may seem curious that the figure of Shrift is depicted as feminine (Malus Angelus calls her "yone olde trat," l. 1578). In the later Middle Ages auricular confession was regarded as a Sacrament that might be administered only by a regularly ordained priest.[41] Shrift, it may therefore be argued, is here merely an instance of personification allegory that is indicative of an abstract idea, in this case Confession. Insistence only on the abstract nature of Shrift would, however, be quite misleading, since she is clearly not merely a mechanically contrived type. Shrift is, after all, an intensely personal experience obligatory for all Christians, and it is normally joined to the common experience of shame that accompanies the confessing of the secrets of the heart--the same sense of shame that accompanies the modern surrogate confession which takes place on the psychiatrist's couch. The iconography of the scene is felt at the same time that it imparts knowledge about man's condition and provides reconciliation to the order of things as established by the Creator. Mankind through remission of sins is *restored* to his innocence, and he is "To Jhesu Crist that deyed on rode" brought back "ageyn ful sadde" (ll. 1526-27). That the feminine should have a role in this should not be surprising, particularly since in medieval thinking the feminine had had a function first of all in the initial act of alienation--an act which has made necessary all subsequent acts of reconciliation, including the one dramatized in *The Castle of Perseverance.*

Following his confession and absolution, Humanum Genus requests to know where he may live "To kepe me fro synne and woo" (l. 1534). Shrift will thus lead him into the Castle of Perseverance where he will remain for safety ("it is strenger thanne any in Fraunce," l. 1553):

> That castel is a precyous place,
> Ful of vertu and of grace;
> Whoso leuyth there hys lyuys space
> No synne schal hym schende.
> (ll. 1555-59)

From these lines we may deduce that the castle is first of all a structure that represents a life of virtue as opposed to the Seven Deadly Sins. It is thus a sacred zone that provides protection for the reconciled soul. A comparison hence may be made to the castle in which Mary Magdalene resides in the Digby play prior to her fall into sin; when she succumbs to evil, she must desert the castle, which has its source in the word *castellum* that signifies Bethany in the Vulgate version of the New Testament.[42]

As a scenic device in the center of the playing area, the castle in *The Castle of Perseverance* is further aligned with path of freedom for the soul, who, as we have seen, must go to the east rather than in any other direction if the result is not to be entrapment by the Deadly Sins. There is no need either here or in the Digby play of *Mary Magdalene* to develop very extensively the argument that the Castle of Virtue thus dramatized and placed on stage should be narrowly symbolic of the Blessed Virgin Mary, who is equated with the symbolic castle in Mirk's *Festial*.[43] Yet the individual who achieves the righteous life over against the temptations of the Deadly Sins is one who nevertheless brings his or her own life (however imperfectly) into line with the model of perfection, which is in fact exemplified for late medieval religion by the Blessed Virgin.

The stage castle utilized in *The Castle of Perseverance* must have been very like the forts pictured in a remarkable series of illuminations painted at Bruges in manuscripts of *La Forteresse de la Foy* (c.1470-80).[44] The miniatures show the figurative castle, usually behind some sort of barricade, as the focal point in the battle between Virtue and Vice (fig. 13). More often than not the castle in these miniatures is extremely simple in construction, with an open area below a romanesque arch in some instances.[45] A structural detail such as this open space beneath an arch may well have been duplicated in *The Castle of Perseverance*, though it is hard to know precisely what was signified in the stage diagram accompanying the play. Richard Southern's inspired reconstruction of the castle's design indeed makes better use of sightlines than would be the case with any design based on the miniatures since he places the structure on stilts, though there is no evidence from the visual arts or iconography to give precise support to his conjectures in this regard.[46] It is, of course, highly unlikely that either the author of the play or the early actors who performed it would have produced a castle design that was particularly innovative, and we also can assume that the structure would have been an adaptation from another source rather than from any extant illustration in an illuminated manuscript. We know, for example, that pavilions, tents, towers, and castles were used for various entertainments out of doors for summer festivals in England,[47] and it is very possible that the principal stage setting for *The Castle of Perseverance* was adapted from the canvas structures that were utilized on such occasions.

But the principal characteristic of the castle in *The Castle of Perseverance* is that it is associated with the Seven Moral Virtues, who literally guard the fortress against the Seven Deadly Sins and serve figuratively as a remedy for them. According to the tradition ultimately inherited from Prudentius, each of the Virtues will be precisely opposed to one of the Deadly Sins--i.e., Humility against Pride, Patience against Wrath, Charity against Envy, Abstinence against Gluttony, Chastity against Lechery, Industry against Sloth, and Generosity against Covetousness. Their reception of Humanum Genus, though imperfect in the text because of a missing leaf following line 1601,[48] is joyous in spite of the subject matter of their speeches, which describe their role in confronting the Deadly Sins and also delineate the protagonist's responsibility in following their precepts. In contrast to the secretly ugly and two-faced Vices, these Virtues are truly "louely and lyt" ladies (l. 1667) who also are health-giving and reconciling in their function. But the reconciliation naturally does not extend to the Vices, and in medieval art such Virtues had been frequently illustrated as triumphing over the personifications of vice (e.g., in the influential drawings of scenes in the *Psychomachia* manuscripts or in further drawings in the *Hortus Deliciarum*[49]), though differences will be found between any examples of the Virtues-Vices conflict that we might wish to compare.[50] The lack of a rigid iconographic tradition in such illustrations must thus be taken into account in any analysis that is undertaken of the dramatic types of the Virtues and Vices as they appear in such a play as *The Castle of Perseverance*.

Occasionally, the Virtues were shown separately from the depictions of the Vices in the art of the Middle Ages, as in the restored thirteenth-century sculptures on the Chapter House portal at Salisbury Cathedral. Here, for example, Charity is giving an article of clothing to a poor person,[51] and though the article being given and the act being performed are in fact the work of the restorer, there is a good possibility in this case that the original design also called for just such a gift to the figure of the impoverished person. The restorer's model was apparently the figure at Laon,[52] but the subject also appears at Amiens.[53] Such an example of generosity is also intended in Charity's speech in *The Castle of Perseverance*. "Al thi doynge as dros is drye," she tells Humanum Genus, unless "in Charyte thou dyth thi dede" (ll. 1604-05). Thus, instead of reacting as the opposing Vice would respond--i.e., envying what little the poor man might have--the figure of Charity on the Salisbury portal represents the kind of person who would naturally give of her own to succor him. Her action is imitative of the Crucifixion, in which Christ was placed on the rood as a prime exemplar of love--i.e., of charity. Indeed, the well of mercy to which Charity refers in line 1610 is actually a fountain of love that is extended to those who will participate in the mysteries of the Sacraments and will commit their lives to works of charity. Reference here to a continental example will also deepen our understanding of the iconography of charity. In the famous series of corbels showing the Virtues and Vices in Uppsala Cathedral in Sweden, the presentation of Charity involves a representation of the phoenix and pelican;[54] the latter image was very popular in both English and continental iconography, for the pelican, which was reputed to pierce its own breast in order to feed its young when they are in danger of starving, is also a standard emblem of Christ's crucifixion.[55] Hence even a symbolic representation tended to illustrate the manner in which human beings need to participate in the imitation of the central acts of history--in this case the Crucifixion--in pursuit of virtue and reconciliation with the divine order.

Paradoxically, the most important of the Virtues is Humility, who is given the first speech among them because she is precisely opposed to Pride, the root of all evil. It is useful here to extend the discussion of the iconography of *The Castle of Perseverance* once again somewhat beyond the limits of the play in order to see how the Virtues and Vices were thought to be related. While the Tree of Good and the Tree of Evil, which are iconographic commonplaces of the medieval period, do not directly find their way into the drama, they nevertheless help us to understand the context in which the Virtues and Vices in the play were regarded. In medieval depictions of the Tree of Good (*Arbor Bona*) and the Tree of Evil (*Arbor Mala*), Humility and Pride are given frequent prominence at the roots of the trees.[56] The Tree of Good, as we might guess, is identified with the tree which brings forth fruit in the parable in *Matthew* 7.6-20; hence in the twelfth-century *Liber Floridus* illuminated in Ghent, this tree is vigorously sprouting leaves and flowers, while the Virtues appear as fruits on the branches. The same manuscript shows the Tree of Evil as a dead or dying tree without flowers and with a minimum of leaves.[57] When we turn to these Trees in later English illuminated manuscripts such as the De Lisle Psalter, we see a Tree of Vices (fol. 128v; see fig. 14) which is also identified directly with the Fall while its root is in fact labeled *Superbia*--i.e., Pride.[58] In contrast, Humility is everywhere symptomatic of the opposite of the Fall. "Dame Meknes," as Humanum Genus calls her in *The Castle of Perseverance*, is possessed of great "myth" or power (l. 1671), which will enable the individual to escape the vengeance that God will visit on the Proud at the Last Day. Conversely, a common representation of Pride shows that figure being hurled down from a horse.[59] Pride is in fact the first Vice which Humanum Genus must give up at the time of his conversion and reconciliation to God, when he is required humbly to submit himself to a different order which will separate him from the destructive forces of alienation that are loose in the cosmos. Further, if we keep in mind the symbolism of the Tree of Good and the Tree of Evil, the one is symptomatic of fertility and fruitfulness and of spiritual riches, while the other is a sign of dryness, of despair, and of death. Appropriately, therefore, it is Humility who welcomes Humanum Genus to the castle, which he enters of his "owyn wylle" (l. 1694). In order that he might be safe in the castle, he will stand "as stylle as ston" (l. 1697) within the mercy which is extended to him there. His life is to be one of contemplation rather than of action, of withdrawal from the world rather than an attempt to reform it.

    The iconography of the Virtues as located in a castle or tower[60] has a long history which it is possible only to review briefly here.

The sources of the idea are very early indeed, for according to a vision described in the *Shepherd of Hermas* in the second century the Church itself is like a tower given support by seven ladies who represent seven Virtues.[61] It has also been pointed out that a scene presented in catacomb art at Naples shows three Virtues assisting in the construction of a tower which is an allegorical representation of the Church.[62] In the twelfth century, in the *Liber Scivias* of Hildegard of Bingen, five Virtues are placed in a tower in the wall of the City of God signifying the historical period between Noah and Moses; in this instance, the tower is again an allegorical one, representing the will of God who is preparing man's salvation.[63] Literary evidence also abounds to illustrate the establishment of the allegorical Castle of Virtue (e.g., the thirteenth-century *Sawles Warde* in Middle English).[64]

Examples of towers and castles defended by ladies in the visual arts, combined with those contained in texts, suggest that there should be further examination in order to trace the relationship between the secular and sacred scenes and to establish more clearly the structure of the iconography as it informs *The Castle of Perseverance*. The secular scene in which the castle of love defended by a lady is attacked because of a love motive seems curiously to blend into the sacred use of the same iconographic type. Of course, the blurring of the line between sacred and secular in this period was fairly common, with Christ's Passion even being compared to the trial endured by a lover-knight who is fighting for his lady (in this instance, the Church and the individual souls of all Christians).[65] In the case of the sacred use of the iconography of the Virtues in the castle, therefore, the meaning should seem clear: virtue takes on a strong and assertively defensive stance against the Vices that human beings otherwise would find attractive in the world. An ivory in the Victoria and Albert Museum which shows the defense of a castle by ladies (mirror case, A.561-1910; fig. 15) may be wholly secular in meaning, but can we say the same about a similar-appearing scene (fig. 16) in the Luttrell Psalter (c.1340)?[66] Feminine figures in the castle shown in this illumination throw down flowers, while another at the top holds a trumpet with a banner. At the right, one knight attempting to climb a ladder in order to scale the walls of the castle is knocked down by a flower. In the center, a knight is ineffectually knocking at the doorway, and another at the right of the doorway is using a crossbow. On the left of the miniature is a group on the attack being pelted with flowers. This illumination appears in the lower margin of the page in association with Psalm 38 (39), *Dixi custodiam*, which takes up the theme of guarding oneself against the dangers of evil:

> I said: I will take heed to my ways: that I sin not with my tongue. I have set a guard to my mouth, when the sinner stood against me. . . . And now what is my hope? is it not the Lord? and my substance is with thee. Deliver thou me from all my iniquities: thou hast made me a reproach to the fool. I was dumb, and I opened not my mouth, because thou hast done it. Remove thy scourges from me. . . . Hear my prayer, O Lord, and my supplication: give ear to my tears. Be not silent: for I am a stranger with thee, and a sojourner as all my fathers were. O forgive me, that I may be refreshed, before I go hence, and be no more. (Verses 2, 8-11, 13-14)

While secular illustrations do appear frequently in the Luttrell Psalter, the miniature that accompanies this psalm would appear to be very relevant to the text of the psalm, which stresses the strong conflict between the stance of the individual and the threatening moral temptations which surround him.

Less certain of identification, at least upon initial examination, may be the castle defended by ladies in the fourteenth-century Peterborough Psalter, fol. 91v. The illustration, which presents a group of women fending off attacking knights, may nevertheless even here have been meant to be more serious than a diversionary scene to amuse a worldly reader.[67] At the very least, it may have been intended to represent the triumph of feminine chastity, in which case the victory would have been against Luxuria, a sin of the Flesh. Two other illuminations by the same artist, known as "Master B," in the Peterborough Psalter may similarly be examples which, though currently identified as secular, are not unrelated to the sacred nature of the accompanying texts. One of these illustrations appears at the bottom of fol. 39v, where on the left a boy and a girl picking (and presumably stealing) cherries may be a reference to Psalm 50 (51) which immediately precedes the illustration: "Turn away thy face from my sins, and blot out all my iniquities" (verse 11). The same underlying idea may also be present on the right side of the illumination, which shows a bear pursuing a monk; the bear may be intended as a symbol of animal passion, particularly of the sexual sort.[68] The other illumination, which takes up a square at the bottom of fol. 47, shows a hunting scene, with the hunter blowing his horn and a hound pursuing various animals--an oblique reference perhaps to verse 24 of Psalm 67 (68), the accompanying psalm: "That thy foot may be dipped in the blood of thy enemies; the tongue of thy dogs be red with the same." This examination of these three miniatures indicates that we cannot any longer assume that the miniature which shows ladies defending a castle in the Peterborough Psalter must simply be a secular illustration.[69] The scene would seem to be more than merely an amusing scene to keep a drowsy patron awake, and further the illumination helps to suggest that the connection we ought to make with regard to the castle in *The Castle of Perseverance* will be with such illustrations attached to the psalms rather than with purely secular art and literature.

The castle in *The Castle of Perseverance* which protects the contemplative Humanum Genus from temptation is in any case indicative of an active defense that will attempt to ward off the enemies of goodness that would alienate him from virtue and devotion. The Virtues are not themselves either passive or silent, for as established by tradition they will successfully fight against those who would attack their values. Not untypical is the continental miniature in the *Speculum Virginum* ascribed to Conrad of Hirsau which shows Humility thrusting a sword into the breast of Pride, who has fallen before her and has dropped his shield.[70] Similarly aggressive is the figure of Faith on the portal of the Chapter House at Salisbury; here the Virtue is in the process of hanging her opposing Vice, Infidelity.[71] The rope, partly a restoration, is being drawn over the gallows by Faith, and extends around the neck of Infidelity, who is blindfolded in a fashion typical of the iconography of Synagoga (cf. fig. 20), a figure normally contrasted to the allegorical representation of the Church.[72] Such an active approach to evil is in the medieval view necessary because vice itself is always busily seeking its ends, which to be sure may be ultimately self-defeating and destructive. This quality of vice is well depicted in the representation of the Tree of Evil at Hoxne, Suffolk, where two devils are sawing through the trunk of the Tree itself. Though now obliterated, the mouth of hell formerly awaited the fall of the Tree.[73] Such is the end of evil and alienation from God and from his Creation. The Tree of Evil is (if we may interpolate from Christ's words in *John* 15.6 about the withered branch that shall be "cast . . . into the fire" on account of its unfruitfulness) a tree which contains within itself the cause of its own destruction, for it is alienated from the life inherent in the Creation.

If, however, the Virtues as depicted in the play seem negative in their hostility to evil, they are nevertheless ultimately positive in their promotion of a correct mental attitude and of good works which will benefit the social order and those living in it in spite of the lack in the drama of any program of reform that might transform that order. At the height of his vice-ridden insolence, Humanum Genus indulges himself in kingly pride and refuses to do the Corporal Acts of Mercy. He is not mindful of the fragile state of a man in the social order, and he refuses to succor those who are in need of charity:

> I schal neuere begger bede
> Mete nyn drynke, be heuene blys;
> Rather or I schulde hym clothe or fede
> He schulde sterue and stynke iwys.
> (ll. 871-74)

Here, then, is the truly life-denying negativism of evil, which refuses to do those things necessary for salvation. Such a person as this risks being among those at the Last Day who will be told to go down into the punishment of the everlasting bonfire.

The binary division of the race--i.e., the division of the race into the followers of Cain and of Abel, of Judas and St. Peter--is, as suggested above, basic to the understanding achieved in *The Castle of Perseverance*, and it is also integral to our interpretation of a wall painting of the Last Judgment (fig. 17) on the west wall of the parish church at Trotton, Sussex, where the evil man (nude and originally phallic) is contrasted with the good man. The evil man is surrounded by the Seven Deadly Sins, which are placed in the mouths of dragons that issue from his body. Among the sins are Pride (at the top, above his head), Gluttony with a jug raised to his mouth (with more to eat and drink both before him and behind him), Avarice seated before a chest and fending off a small demon with a fork, Sloth lying on a bed (his prayer beads and prayer book have been cast aside), Wrath who is stabbing himself, Lechery, and Envy.[74] These sins, which are placed over a much faded hell mouth, are contrasted with the good man on the other side of the painting. In roundels surrounding the decorously clad good man are the Corporal Acts of Mercy as well as the remains of scrolls which listed the Seven Virtues, though the series of Virtues differs from the order set forth in *The Castle of Perseverance*.[75] Above each of the figures of the evil and good men is an angel either turning away or accepting a nude soul into heaven. The lesson is a very simple one: he who does the Seven Deadly Sins and at the same time fails to perform the Corporal Acts of Mercy (while also neglecting the Seven Virtues) will at the Last Day be placed in serious trouble and in danger of being damned.

In *The Castle of Perseverance*, when Malus Angelus finds that he has lost control of Humanum Genus, he swears by "Belyals bryth bonys" (l. 1715) that the representative of humankind shall be brought out of the fortification through the efforts of the Three Enemies of Man and the Seven Deadly Sins, who will join him in attacking the castle. His messenger to the World, the Flesh, and the Devil, will be Backbiter (*Detractio*), who is also known as Flepyrgebet, a name that recurs in *King Lear* III.iv.18.[76] Backbiter, who is memorable for his role in reporting information, is indeed an appropriate carrier of the news that Humanum Genus is reformed. He had appeared in the platea while Humanum Genus was being clothed by Folly and Lust-Liking, and with his first words in the play had announced himself as a mischief maker and vice figure who tells "talys vntrewe" (l. 654). He is a distributor of false stories or, as in this instance, of stories told with a false motive in mind, and in any case his true object is to stir up trouble. By nature he is two-faced, speaking "fayre beforn and fowle behynde" (l. 664). "Fleterynge and flaterynge is my lessun," he says (l. 669), and he is more crafty than a fox, a creature whose duplicity was, of course, proverbial.[77] He carries with him a letter box containing "letterys of defamacyoun" (l. 671). When Humanum Genus was newly clothed, he had announced himself as his "page" to point him to Covetousness' scaffold. Following Humanum Genus' reformation, as Backbiter sets out to go first to the scaffold of the Flesh, he rejoices that he is able to "make men masyd and mad/ And euery man to kyllyn odyr/ Wyth a sory chere" (ll. 1739-41). Hence he is utterly delighted when the news he brings sets off a violent reaction as Belial beats Pride, Envy, and Wrath upon the ground in a scene that in its comedy is theatrically effective. It is also "good game," Backbiter insists (l. 1823), when Gluttony, Sloth, and Lechery are beaten in the platea by Flesh, and further when the World beats Covetousness.[78] This mischievous devil is also capable of blowing a horn (a trumpet?) and hence is related to the class of demons who play wind instruments--i.e., instruments that have been associated since antiquity with unruly emotions rather than with the intellect, which in contrast would more appropriately be reflected in string music.[79]

Preparation for the siege of the Castle of Virtue begins very rapidly, for the World insists that such "bycchys" as the Seven Virtues shall not "dwellyn in my londe" (ll. 1884, 1889). The banners of battle are raised, and in their crude anger the Three Enemies of Man prepare for a conflict in which they will be assisted by the Seven Deadly Sins. Pride in his haughty way vows to give "Meknesse myschanse" and to "bothe clatyr and clowte" her "On hyr ars, raggyd and row" (ll. 1931-33). The scatological matter and what actors call "crotch jokes" are carefully chosen, since they are appropriate to the powers of darkness and dirt, though as aimed at the Virtues who are noted for their purity they are in fact ironic. When Gluttony insists that he shall set up such a smoke screen that the Virtues "schul schytyn for fere" (l. 1968), his impolite words actually foreshadow what will happen to himself at the hands of Abstinence, who beats him all over, "toppe and tayl" (l. 2383). The preparation for battle culminates in a rousing speech by the evil angel, who addresses the Three Enemies of Man in turn after all have assembled in the platea. Of those who set forth to besiege the castle, however, the most impressive surely must ultimately be Belial, who is described below the play's stage plan: "and he that schal pley belyal loke that he haue gunnepowdyr brennynge In pypys in hys handys and in hys erys and in hys ars whanne he gothe to batayl."[80] Nevertheless, the sparks and the traditional smoke associated with demons will not carry the day when he and his company attack the castle.

As in the illumination in the Luttrell Psalter (fig. 16), the castle in *The Castle of Perseverance* is strongly attacked by figures more formidably armed than the ladies who defend it. In the first stage of the attack, Wrath is equipped with stones that he will "slynge" at the castle (l. 2112), while Envy carries a bow. Humility, however, holds a banner that, since it is marked with the emblem of the Crucifixion, counters the banner of Pride, while Patience and Charity throw down roses upon their enemies. The flowers are amazingly effective, for the three assailants are badly hurt. As weapons, the roses are clearly not so different from the emblem on the banner held by Humility, since they too represent the Passion of Christ in this context.[81] The dramatic effect upon the Sins may be said to be similar to the scene carved much earlier on a Norman font at Southrop; here we see Wrath, who has been beaten by Patience with her scourge upon the buttocks, rubbing herself in pain.[82]

The second wave of attackers is led by Flesh. Gluttony, who more usually carries a container for wine or beer, here holds a firebrand on his shoulder, while Lechery carries the coals that she uses to "make a fer in mans towte" or genital region (l. 2289). Against Gluttony, Abstinence holds up the bread of the Sacrament, while Chastity, who grasps the rod of chastity, calls upon the Blessed Virgin to "qwenche that fowle hete" (l. 2303). Obviously the rod that appears as a prop held by Chastity is an instrument representing power over the fire of Lechery, for this Virtue has genuine authority when contrasted to the fraudulence of the unchaste allegorical woman whom she opposes. The final member of this group of sins is Sloth, who attempts to divert the "watyr of grace" from the moat around the castle of virtue (l. 2329) only to be himself diverted from the task by Industry (*Solicitudo*) with her prayer beads. In an exchange which certainly calls for slapstick designed to obtain a hearty laugh from the audience, this Sin is not only hurt on his "skallyd skulle" but also, it would appear, in his "ballokys" or testicles (ll. 2399, 2403). In each instance, the weapon chosen by the Virtues is iconographically correct, and the result of the battle is a comic defeat in the playing area for the Seven Deadly Sins and the Three Enemies of Man.

The success, however, stops when the seventh Sin, more wily than the rest, makes an appeal directly to Humanum Genus in spite of the objections of and to the dismay of Generosity, whose task it is to oppose this Sin. Because now that he is an old man Humanum Genus is more susceptible to avarice, he will submit himself to Covetousness and will go away with him out of the Castle of Virtue. "He wyl forsake this precyous place," the good angel laments, "And drawe ageyn to dedly synne" (ll. 2546-47). Humility, as the leader of the Virtues, is unfortunately unable at this point to do anything about the defection of Humanum Genus, since "God hath gouyn hym a fre wylle" (l. 2560). The great temptation has been the necessity he has felt to gather around him more wealth for his old age; he is convinced that Covetousness is correct when he tells him, "If thou be pore and nedy in elde,/ Thou schalt oftyn euyl fare" (ll. 2529-30). Paradoxically, as Patience warns, he is in fact brewing "hymselfe a byttyr galle" (ll. 2576-77). Abstinence calls him a fool who seems to be subjecting himself ultimately to hell fire, and Chastity suggests that there will be a day when Humanum Genus will be more in need of prayer beads than of worldly goods.[83]

But Humanum Genus persists in pursuing worldly goods nevertheless, though "In hys moste nede" the World "schal hym fayle" (l. 2698). Covetousness will take him to his cupboard from which he will give the world's riches to him. The location of the cupboard is indicated on the page containing the diagram at the conclusion of the text of the play in the manuscript: "Coveytyse copbord be the beddys feet schal be at the ende of the castel."[84] Southern wonders "what can Covetyse's cupboard be? And why, if it is Covetyse's, should it be under the Castle of all places, and not on his scaffold? Again, if this is true, why specify its relation to the bed, and why must the 'cupboard' be especially at the bed's foot?"[85] Answers to these questions can only be suggested by iconography. A chest or similar container for riches is a regular item in illustrations of avarice in the visual arts. Such a formerly locked chest appears at the foot of the bed of the dying miser in Hieronymus Bosch's *Death and the Miser* in the National Gallery, Washington, D.C.[86] The symbolic chest is also prevalent in English iconography. At Blythburgh, Suffolk, a benchend shows Avarice sitting on a closed chest.[87] An open chest appears in the wall painting at Trotton as an attribute of Avarice, who is seated and fending off a small mischievous demon that carries a fork.[88] Both the chest and a devil, who in this case is flying, have been noted in connection with this sin on the Tree of the Seven Deadly Sins in the fourteenth-century wall painting at Bardwell, Suffolk.[89] At Crostwight, Norfolk, Avarice appears under the weight of bags of money, while at Hoxne this sin holds a moneybag and is removing coins from a box.[90] In *The Castle of Perseverance*, Covetousness takes a thousand marks from the "copboard" and gives them to Humanum Genus with the admonition that he should be selfish about his use of this money. As Humanum Genus takes the bag of money, he vows to use it in the manner of good "husbondry"; ironically, he says that he will "hyde this gold vndyr the grownde" (ll. 2739-42) like a seed that cannot grow because it is sterile.

Humanum Genus' plan to bury the thousand marks is reminiscent of the parable of the talents in *Matthew* 25, a chapter rich in eschatological resonances. In this parable, the alienated servant to whom only one talent was given buried it in the ground with unprofitable results; for his poor stewardship, he is thrown "out into the exterior darkness"--a location where there "shall be weeping and gnashing of teeth" (*Matt.* 25.30). Even if his plan to bury his gold is not literally carried out, the iconographic context indicates that Humanum Genus has become the archetypal old miser, in his alienation hoarding up riches and never having enough. All thoughts of the Corporal Acts of Mercy and of reconciliation with God have evaporated from his mind, and he thinks only about himself and the prosperity which insulates him from the reality of his approaching end. His wealth is only an illusion since he misuses it, while the Corporal Acts would have stood him in better stead. As Truth explains during the debate of the Four Daughters of God, Humanum Genus is not worthy of mercy because

> ... he wolde neuere the hungry
> Neythyr clothe nor fede,
> Ner drynke gyf to the thrysty,
> Nyn pore men helpe at nede.
> For if he dyd non of these, forthy
> In heuene he getyth no mede.
> So seyth the gospel.
> For he hathe ben vnkynde
> To lame and to blynde
> In helle he schal be pynde.
> So is resun and skyl.
> (ll. 3472-82)

It is as if in response to Humanum Genus' petition that he might have "More and more" (l. 2773) that "drery Dethe" arrives in the playing area to summon him to account after he has misspent most of his life. Death, of course, is the great leveller before whose dart no one may stand: all are alike variable service at his table. He is the gruesome figure who appears in the Dance of Death illustrations that were so popular in the fifteenth century both in England and on the continent.[91] By Death's hand, Humanum Genus is wounded for the second time in the play, and as that first wound was sustained for his spiritual health, so this one is destined to take away his physical health. As we have long known, the World will not assist him but rather will be pleased at the death and damnation of another of his followers; "Thus haue I seruyd here-beforn," says World, "A hundryd thousand moo" (ll. 2880-81).

The World, however, has committed one further act of malevolence: he has already given Humanum Genus' wealth to another--to a stranger, who has no respect for the protagonist and is anxious only to pocket his goods. Such an episode in the play merits special attention since, as Riggio has pointed out, the more affluent members of the social order of the time were preoccupied with inherited land and wealth.[92] Humanum Genus, intended as representative of his time and region, reminds us of the words of the psalmist: "He storeth up: and he knoweth not for whom he shall gather these things" (*Ps.* 38.7).[93] The name of the stranger who will be his heir and who is so anxious to have him gone is "I Wot Neuere Whoo" (l. 2968). This unpleasant intruder is neither kin nor friend. He acts like a devil, though it seems more likely in the play that he merely affects demonic behavior. Riggio has suggested that he might be a "sekatour" or executor, against whom Humanum Genus has been warned by the Virtues (l. 1660),[94] but the explicit distinction made between executors and the heir in the banns (ll. 102-04) seems effectively to scotch this otherwise attractive suggestion. In any case, the lesson of the scene is the same as that of Bosch's *Death and the Miser*, which shows a devil apparently stealing a large bag of money, while a man at the foot of the bed is assisted by another small devil to take goods from the chest.[95]

Humanum Genus' death in bed presents us with a scene commonly depicted in the visual arts.[96] Like Bosch's miser who is sitting up in bed and, though still attracted to wealth, is having his sight directed toward the crucifix in the upper window through which also a ray of light is entering the room, Humanum Genus seems to know that he is dying. Such knowledge of one's approaching end appears to have been quite usual among people living in pre-modern times.[97] As visual representations from both the continent and England show, the dying person normally had his family and friends about him, sometimes even when he was confessing his sins to a priest for the last time in his life. In the Egmont Psalter (c.1460) in the Pierpont Morgan Library, the dying man with his hands together in the position of prayer is absolved by a Dominican friar inside the enclosure which is his bed. At the left outside the enclosure, there is a group of four other religious who are apparently friars, while a woman (the man's wife, or a maid?) prepares some food at the fireplace. At the right are eight lay persons, presumably friends and members of the man's family.[98] Sometimes in medieval illustrations the family and friends are resigned to the approaching death, and at other times grief is in evidence among them.[99] But Humanum Genus on his deathbed is isolated and alone, except for the intrusion of the insufferable stranger who has come for his wealth. Not even his guardian angel comes to his side during his ordeal, which is intended to provide for the audience a vicarious experience of life's termination in death. Humanum Genus begins his last speech: "Now, good men, takythe example at me./ Do for youreself whyl ye han spase" (ll. 2995-96). Visually, the death scene involves careful concentration of focus undisturbed by other characters; the protagonist, hoping for grace even in spite of his failure to live the life of faith throughout his entire earthly existence, is lying on the bed, perhaps with his shirt thrown aside so that the bare white skin of his chest will be exposed as a symbol of the fragility of the body. And with his last gasp he cries: "I putte me in Goddys mercy" (l. 3007).

But this is not yet the end of the play, for though Humanum Genus' body is dead, his soul is not. The note under the diagram of the castle describes the staging: "Mankyndeis bed schal be vndyr the castel and ther schal the sowle lye vndyr the bed tyl he schal ryse and pleye."[100] The illusion that is attempted in the play at this point involves the separation of the soul from the body--an event that, as noted above, ought to be visualized rather as it is illustrated in the dialogue "Of the Seven Ages" in British Library MS. Add. 37,049 (fig. 11) except that in the play no guardian angel rushes down to claim the soul for heaven when it issues from the mouth of the dying man.[101] Instead, the soul, though he complains about the body that had held him imprisoned, must turn to the good angel and beg for help against his dread of the devil's sadistic treatment if he must go to hell. And indeed, as the good angel must tell him, he seems destined for hell where, the bad angel is delighted to say, he will burn (in "bolnynnge bondys thou schalt brenne," he is told): "In pycke and ter to grone and grenne;/ Thou schalt lye drenkelyd as a movs" (ll. 3076, 3078-79). Hell paradoxically will be at once a "dongion" (l. 3100) and hot. Precisely the latter extreme is the one that is most frequently encountered in the visual arts in England in the Middle Ages. Hell cauldrons were prevalent in the romanesque period,[102] and following the invention of the blast furnace its technology was commonly imagined within hell as the source of the most intense heat applied to wicked souls. Thus, for example, in the *Holkham Bible Picture Book* (fol. 34) the deeper recesses of hell are visualized in terms of the blast furnace where the most intense heat is being applied to the souls seated in a cauldron over the demonic fire while a grisly devil stirs among them with his flesh hook.

As in illustrations of the Last Judgment, the punishment of the soul begins even before the gates of hell are entered. Malus Angelus beats the soul with his club, which possibly is the same type of instrument of stuffed and painted canvas that was apparently utilized for devils in the mystery plays.[103] When he takes the soul to hell, he perhaps does so by picking him up and placing him astride his neck on his shoulders as in the final illumination in the *Holkham Bible Picture Book* (fol. 42^v). Similarly, in the West Window illustrating the Doom at Fairford, a blue devil carries a reluctant soul on his shoulder; the soul imploringly stretches out its arms toward St. Michael (fig. 18). A red demon in the same window has thrown another damned soul over his shoulder and is carrying it off toward a furnace, which in this instance is an oven with a bellows of the type used by glass blowers.[104] In the play, however, it would appear that the bad angel takes the soul to the scaffold of the Devil where he presumably suffers the intense pains of purgatory.

Humanum Genus' soul now will hang in the balance while the debate of the Four Daughters of God takes place. Based on the account in Psalm 84 (85), these figures were regarded as intimately associated with the process of salvation.

> Wilt thou be angry with us for ever: or wilt thou extend thy wrath from generation to generation? Thou wilt turn, O God, and bring us to life: and thy people shall rejoice in thee. Shew us, O Lord, thy mercy; and grant us thy salvation. I will hear what the Lord God will speak in me: for he will speak peace unto his people: And unto his saints: and unto them that are converted to the heart. Surely his salvation is near to them that fear him: that glory may dwell in our land. Mercy and truth have met each other: justice and peace have kissed. Truth is sprung out of the earth: and justice hath looked down from heaven. For the Lord will give goodness: and our earth shall yield her fruit. (*Ps.* 84.6-13)

In the *Meditations on the Life of Christ*, the debate and reconciliation of the Four Daughters of God are closely linked with the preparation for the Incarnation (and, therefore, with the Annunciation).[105] This emphasis is also present in the N-town cycle, which alone among the extant mystery cycles includes this episode, known as the Parliament of Heaven.[106] The same general understanding of the meaning of the Four Daughters of God is contained in Grosseteste's *Chateau d'amour*, translated into Middle English as the *Castel of Loue*.[107] *The Castle of Perseverance*, however, sets forth a different context for the story, for the debate is about the soul of a single representative layman who happens to be all too typical, and it takes place after the work of the Incarnation and Crucifixion has been completed.

In the play, the argument begins in the platea with Mercy's assertion that, because of the shedding of blood by God's Son on the cross, "It hadde ben satysfaccion goode/ For al Mankyndys werke" (ll. 3149-50). Mercy, who wears a mantle of pure white,[108] is rightly man's "waschynge-well" (l. 3145). Justice, dressed in her red mantle,[109] objects, since in fairness Humanum Genus does not deserve to be given immortal life: "As he hath browyn [i.e., brewed], lete hym drynke" (l. 3161). Truth, wearing "sad grene,"[110] then agrees with this harsh verdict, while Peace "al in blake"[111] objects to the idea of man being judged "to helle" (l. 3206) when God himself has performed the work of salvation in order to make reconciliation possible. "For hys loue that deyed on tre," Peace tells Truth and Justice, "Late saue Mankynd fro al peryle/ And schelde hym fro myschaunsse" (ll. 3209-11). At Peace's suggestion, they will attempt to resolve their differences by appealing to God, whose scaffold in the East now becomes the focal point of the action of the play. As we would surely expect, Mercy's plea for the soul of Humanum Genus is indeed deeply felt and is presented with strong emphasis on the idea of the fortunate fall. Justice will remain unconvinced since Humanum Genus had forsaken his baptismal vows in adulthood in favor of a dissolute life with the Seven Deadly Sins to which he was tempted by his evil angel; he even thought that he would live indefinitely in his alienated state--an opinion that he held until he became caught up in the Dance of Death. "Ouyrlate he callyd Confescion," Justice complains; "Ouerlyt was hys contricioun;/ He made neuere satisfaccioun" (ll. 3427-29). The debate continues until Peace, taking note of the reason for man's creation in the beginning as a replacement for the order of fallen angels, urges a reconciliation: "Lete vs foure systerys kys,/ And restore Man to blis,/ As was Godys ordenaunce" (ll. 3519-21).

The reconciliation of the Four Daughters of God, reflecting precisely the words of the psalm which describes the meeting of Mercy and Truth as well as the kiss of Justice and Peace, is the culmination of the scene and the core of its iconography. Reference may usefully be made to an earlier English illumination, in a twelfth-century Bible in the Lambeth Library: here Mercy (with a jar of ointment) and Truth appear in a roundel formed by the branches of a tree under the Blessed Virgin's right arm, while Justice (with the traditional scales) and Peace appear in a similar roundel under the Virgin's left arm.[112] Mary, who represents the principle of mercy at work in the Incarnation, stands at the center of the illumination as the trunk of the tree that culminates at the top with Christ, who is surrounded by doves. The tree has as its root the figure of Jesse, who is sleeping at the bottom. Later illustrations showing the Four Daughters of God (e.g., a fifteenth-century manuscript Book of Hours in the Pierpont Morgan Library, MS. 179)[113] are likely to show God as the Trinity in heaven above them, and they are also not always illustrated at precisely the moment of their reconciliation.

In the drama, God approves the reconciliation of the Four Daughters, and sends them to release Humanum Genus from "yone fende" (l. 3576). The confrontation with the bad angel is very brief, with the Daughters ascending to his scaffold--presumably, as noted above, the stage shared with Belial--and then bringing back the soul which has been in captivity. Malus Angelus must be ordered to release the soul, whereupon he is ordered to go to hell where he must dwell and "In bras and brimston to welle" (l. 3593). The soul is then brought back to the scaffold where God sits on his throne; they ascend the scaffold in preparation for the invitation to sit at the right hand of the deity. The tableau is one of comfort to an audience which presumably fears the final reckoning that is to come at the Last Day, though at the same time God insists comfortingly that there will be a careful sifting out of the good and the bad when the fearful day arrives. God is indeed a merciful God, as the play teaches, but his mercy is not endless. There will be those who will be placed on the left side of God and consigned to hell forever and ever. The ending of the drama is thus deliberately designed to remind the viewers of not only the end of individual human life on this earth but also the end of history itself. The last lines, spoken directly to the audience, are very revealing with regard to the intent of the play:

> Thus endyth oure gamys.
> To saue you fro synnynge,
> Evyr at the begynnynge
> Thynke on youre last endynge.
> (ll. 3645-48)

Appropriately, the very last line of the drama thereafter gives the incipit for the *Te Deum laudamus*, a liturgical item that was sung here just as it was sung not only by the orders of angels moving back and forth around the heavenly throne in the Creation play in the York Corpus Christi cycle but also at the end of the Towneley play of the Last Judgment.[114]

The Castle of Perseverance, a play which moves through all the stages along life's way and which re-creates the life of the individual in terms of the historical predicament of the race, thus concludes with a musical item of praise to the Maker of all things. The *Te Deum* brings the play-acting of the drama to a close and further ends the action in a harmony that affirms the value of reconciliation with God and with the order of his universe. The theatrical experience has been varied and extensive, moving from serious moments of conflict to unbridled slapstick, but the focus has never failed to remain on the aspect of potential and realized alienation and on the remedy for such a condition. The drama is, when considered from the standpoint of its purpose, didactic, but it also does not fail to draw its audience into the action and to achieve a liveliness that makes it effective as theatrical experience.

III

WISDOM: THE ICONOGRAPHY OF MYSTICISM

The text of *Wisdom* is characterized by diction which is heavily aureate and by a structure which is formalized and symmetrical. If, as Gail McMurray Gibson has speculated, *Wisdom* was staged in the Abbot's dining hall before King Edward IV at the Benedictine Abbey of Bury St. Edmunds when he visited in 1469,[1] the monastic and royal context would determine that this play should be differentiated in tone and design from *Mankind* and *The Castle of Perseverance*, the other dramas now collected in the same manuscript. Thus when produced on stage *Wisdom* demands an acting style which is substantially different from that required by the other Macro moralities, and it also opens up a quite different aspect of late medieval iconography--i.e., its direct connection with certain devotional practices involving images. Finally, it is a drama which visualizes human psychology more specifically than do the other Macro plays.

Peter Happé has remarked upon witnessing a production of *Wisdom* at Winchester Cathedral in 1981 that "This kind of theater is primarily iconographic and symbolic, inviting us to observe the relationship between its many elements, and barely allowing for the sequence, the movement in time which is indispensable to most forms of drama."[2] And David Bevington argues that this variety of drama "derives its theatrical form from the visualizing of metaphor, from the concretizing of homiletic and scriptural proposition."[3] Such a play must be less "realistic" in presentation in spite of being designed to be acted indoors in a dining hall, and will even demand a different manner of speaking by the actors--the Winchester production in 1981 was reported to have adopted an "elevated style"--than we we would expect to be used in the other moralities in the Macro manuscript. W. A. Davenport has observed how the first scene of the play involves "a tableau, which could be taken from a medieval manuscript or stained-glass window, of Christ in majesty," and he indicates (quite correctly) that the entire play is at once "a poetic drama and a set of patterns and pictures."[4] Valuable as such suggestions are for our understanding of the play, it is nevertheless necessary to go beyond these general comments to understand more exactly the mechanisms by which visual images are given meaning and function in a play that partakes of the Christian mysticism so widespread in England in the late Middle Ages.

It will be seen upon examination that visually *Wisdom* is structured about a devotional image through which the divine *Logos* may be approached and experienced by the soul. As we might expect for a play which was inspired not only by monastic ideals but also by the Christian mysticism of the West, the *Logos* is perceived through the visible figure of Wisdom as at once transcendent and inhering in the order of things: the *Logos* is the goal to be desired above all things, and yet it gives structure and meaning to all that exists in the here and now. Wisdom as a character in the play is hence not only Christ, the divine-human man who is the Bridegroom desired as the object of the soul's union in the life hereafter, but also "the image of [the Father's] goodnes" (l. 32); as such, he functions as a devotional image to which the soul, Anima, and presumably also the audience will repond with all the warmth demanded by late medieval piety. The description of the character at the opening of the play is remarkably full, and could well have been in part modelled, as Davenport appears to suggest,[5] on the transcendent image of the Christ in Majesty in the visual arts:

> Fyrst enteryde WYSDOME in a ryche purpull clothe of golde wyth a mantyll of the same ermynnyde wythin, hawynge abowt hys neke a ryall hood furred wyth ermyn, wpon hys hede a cheweler [i.e., a wig] wyth browys, a berde of golde of sypres curlyd, a ryche imperyall crown therwpon sett wyth precyus stonys and perlys, in hys leyfte honde a balle of golde wyth a

cros therwppon and in hys ryght honde a regall schepter.... (*s.d.* at l. 1)

This figure of the crowned and royally attired Christ which dominates the play is one that would have been very familiar to all in the fifteenth century. The crown, the emblems of Christ's power, and his gold beard would all have been well known from the visual arts. The gold beard, along with a gold face, is present, for example, in painted glass of c.1430 now in York Minster,[6] while the crown would have been worn by the Second Person of the Trinity in the ubiquitous representations of the Coronation of the Virgin, a popular scene that suffered much from Protestant iconoclasm, though fortunately many examples survive. In one such example in an alabaster carving from the latter half of the fifteenth century now in the Castle Museum, Nottingham, Christ's elaborate crown blends with the crown of thorns,[7] a detail that is frequent in other alabaster representations and that also appears, for example, in painted glass at Holy Trinity, Goodramgate, York.[8]

Emblems of royal power held by Christ are inherited from examples of the transcendent Christ in Majesty, such as the twelfth-century wall painting in St. Gabriel's Chapel, Canterbury Cathedral, where the Western image of the Savior of the World is shown in most impressive form with the figure of Christ encircled with light and supported by angels.[9] A panel of English embroidery from the fourteenth century now in the Victoria and Albert Museum illustrates a Christ with a nimbus holding an orb with a cross; his bare feet protrude from under his rich robes. This panel, which has affinities with East Anglian book illumination,[10] was perhaps part of an altar frontal and hence it illustrates the continuing presence of this transcendent image of Christ in Majesty, as does at least one example in English alabaster from c.1400.[11] However, other kinds of representations which stressed the presence of Christ among men along with his transcendent power tended to be immensely more popular in the fifteenth century. The Christ of these devotional images was normally much more accessible to the experience of the worshipper than the more remote transcendent Christ, but such images also suffered greatly from iconoclasm since they were especially the targets of iconophobic Protestant zeal in England.

It is unfortunate that the Protestant Reformation in England swept away so much of the evidence from art that would be most helpful for studying precisely the kind of images that are allied to the function of Wisdom in the Macro play.[12] Protestant and rationalist prejudices have also until recently hindered scholars from fully appreciating the significance of popular devotion extended to such images or of their function in the experiencing of mystical Christianity in the late Middle Ages. Because of the historical distance which separates us today from late medieval religious practice, it may be useful to identify the attitudes toward images that were prevalent during that period. Such attitudes are an extension of the pre-medieval defense of images: "The utterly unlearned regard statues as wood and stone, just as those who do not understand written letters look upon monuments as stones and on tablets as bits of wood and on books as woven papyrus."[13] To be sure, many examples of statues intended for devotion (e.g., the popular alabasters from Nottingham, York, and other English workshops) and paintings, including the kind of imported Flemish work that was available, remain extant, though the majority of these in England were destroyed by religious zeal. Relatively recent research[14] has established the manner in which these images were regarded throughout Western Europe--i.e., as essentially the most efficient way by which contact may be made with the deity, otherwise difficult of access, and his saints. The image in the visual arts--and also, we may add, in the drama--provided a window through which the individual might see that which is more true than what the physical eye might perceive. As Nilus the Scholastic had indicated in the sixth century, "the image leads us up to the intellectual memory of heavenly beings."[15] Though by the fifteenth century popular devotion had added new elements in its apprehension of the divine or sacred image, this understanding of the image as a channel to the deity and his saints remained, and it is crucial for a proper interpretation of the iconography of *Wisdom*, which utilizes the devotional image for the purpose of explaining the structure and practice of mystical religion.

While the use of the devotional image does not extend to the earliest practice of the Church, the practice is nevertheless very early. It is well known that the adoption of this kind of image was not entirely without controversy. In the rejection of iconoclasm in the Eastern Church, the Council of Nicea in 787 affirmed the use of religious pictures "of our Lord God and Savior, Jesus Christ, or our spotless Sovereign Lady, the holy Mother of God, or the holy angels and holy and venerable men."[16] The canon adopted by the council continued:

> For each time that we see their representation in an image, each time, while gazing upon them, we are made to remember the prototypes, we grow to love them more, and we are even more induced to worship them by kissing them and by witnessing our veneration (*proskynesis*), not the true adoration (*latreia*) which, according to our faith, is proper only to the one divine nature, but in the same way as we venerate the image of the precious and vivifying cross, the holy Gospel and other sacred objects which we honor with incense and candles according to the pious custom of our forefathers. For the honor rendered to the image goes to its prototype, and the person who venerates an icon, venerates the person represented on it.[17]

Though for the Western Church the official doctrine has often been said to be that religious pictures and images were merely the books of the unlearned, the Eastern idea of the devotional image did make itself very strongly felt through all Christendom prior to the Reformation. To dismiss the devotional image out of hand as mere superstition will not assist in the better understanding of the visual element in late medieval drama. Devotion of this kind was apparently expected as one aspect of the audience response to the great civic cycles such as the ones at York, Chester, and Coventry, where persons are said to have wept pious tears and to have earned indulgences while watching the plays that dramatized the most sacred scenes in Christian history.[18] The honor and devotion directed at an image in a play are in effect passed on to the God or saint who is represented. Such devotion was very highly regarded, for it formed the most important way by which a person could achieve the hope that would lift him or her out of a life cut off from participation in religious experiences leading ultimately to the transcendent God. If we may draw upon a term popularized by

Victor Turner, the individual members of the audience may be said to have found in the moving and living images of the plays an experience of *liminality* that temporarily separated them from their ordinary lives.[19]

For defense of image theology in the late Middle Ages, the most powerful argument at hand was that Christ himself in taking on human form had presented himself in the likeness of a man and had also actually shared the human condition. Since God, while necessarily remaining mysterious, had shown himself to human eyes through the Incarnation, men should therefore feel especially free to use representations of this human form in their devotions. In *Wisdom*, it is the revealed God--the Second Person of the Trinity--who confronts the the soul and its faculties, for it is his image that is believed to communicate the highest knowledge to those who would enter into a relationship with him.[20] The idea of visual confrontation with the image, through which God is revealed, is thus crucial to our understanding of the play, its allegory, its iconography, and its mysticism.

Behind the image of Wisdom in the play there is additionally the long tradition of Wisdom literature that has been discussed by Joseph Green.[21] This literature was, in turn, of considerable importance for the mystical writers of the later Middle Ages, and certain of their writings, especially Henry Suso's *Orologium Sapientiae*, Walter Hilton's *Scale of Perfection* and *Epistle on the Mixed Life*, and the *Novem Virtutes* formerly attributed to Richard Rolle, served as sources for the author of *Wisdom*.[22] The identification between Christ and Wisdom in the play and in its sources owes much to the first chapter of St. John's Gospel which identifies the Second Person of the Trinity as the *Logos* or Word who existed before all worlds. He is the creator of all earthly forms and the author of all life. He is also light, the symbol of spiritual illumination which is capable in mystical experience of flooding the mind; "I am foundon lyghte wythowt comparyson," Wisdom says in the play, "Off sterrys aboue all the dysposicyon,/ Forsothe of lyght the very brightnes,/ Merowre of the dyvyne domynacyon,/ And the image of hys [i.e., God's] goodnes" (ll. 28-32). Unlike the saints who are understood to reflect the divine light (iconographically emblemized in their haloes), Christ in his function as Wisdom is believed to be the absolute source of light which shines in the darkness of this world.[23] This is the reason for the mandorla that encircles Christ in representations of Christ in Majesty (e.g., in the early wall painting in St. Gabriel's Chapel at Canterbury to which reference has been made above[24]) or in certain other scenes which include him. While it is fairly certain that the frontal view of Christ familiar from the Christ in Majesty would have been retained by the actor playing Wisdom as he confronts Anima or the audience, the drama adds an element that is distinctly late medieval to the iconography. At the end of the play, Wisdom refers feelingly to his experience of the Passion, which was necessary if he was to atone for man's sins. But the details of his suffering are significant: he "tastyde the drynke mengylde wyth gall" and felt the "smerte" of pain (ll. 1100-01). He continues:

> My handys sprede abrode to halse thi swyre;
> My fete naylyde to abyde wyth the, swet herte;
> My hert clowyn for thi loue most dere;
> Myn hede bowhede down to kys the here;
> My body full of holys, as a dovehows.
> (ll. 1102-06)

The emphasis is on how these painful things were experienced for men and women whose souls might thus be redeemed and "reformyde" (l. 1107). Such a stance was commonly taken by the Savior in medieval lyrics that have Christ as the speaker (either as *imago pietatis* or from the cross) who emotionally describes what he has done for mankind.[25] In *Wisdom*, it is inconceivable that the reference to hands, feet, and wounded body would have been ignored in the visual tableau of the play. Further, in a manner quite uncharacteristic of the Christ in Majesty in the visual arts, these wounds would have been very visible and perhaps marked with the appearance of fresh blood; further, attention may well have been called to them through appropriate hand gestures. Fifteenth-century art in England made much of the pains of the Passion, which are also very often at this time central to the devotional experience. Thus, an illustration in a manuscript from Norfolk written in 1405 and containing Michael de Massa's *On the Passion of Our Lord* (Bodl. MS. 758, fol. 1) shows the Crucifixion with Christ's body wounded from head to foot from the scourging.[26] But the showing of the wounds in hands, feet, and body is more specifically associated with the Image of Pity (*imago pietatis*) in which the body is displayed as a devotional image, often placed above the tomb from which the Resurrection took place.[27] Such a display seems to have influenced the presentation on stage in *Wisdom*, which thus reflected an important iconographic element of the late medieval Passion devotion here combined with mystical theology. From the opening of the play, therefore, Wisdom is an "image of [God's] goodnes" (l. 32) *because* he reflects the suffering that the Second Person of the Trinity has experienced on behalf of men and women whose souls are the object of divine love.

The principal visual focus on stage is provided by the regal figure of Wisdom. Anima, however, functions as a second point of focus. Theatrically, the two characters are balanced against each other, one representing stability and permanence, the other involving potential either for the retention of devotional focus directed at Wisdom or for falling away from that which ought to be regarded as the center of existence. The play's audience, monastic or lay, could be said to have been invited to participate in the soul's angle of vision, though in any early performance in a monastery, even under the more relaxed conditions of a dining hall, there is not likely to have been much approval of behavior which departs from accepted standards.

The meeting in the play of Wisdom and Anima draws on yet another iconographic model which was very important for the mystics of the Church but which has been barely alluded to above. This model is the allegory of the Bridegroom and the Bride, interpreted as Christ and the Church, in the *Song of Songs*.[28] Wisdom, identified with Christ, hence is not only both God and man, but also "Spows of the chyrche and wery patrone" given in marriage to "eche chose sowle" (ll. 15-16). The language, especially at the opening of the play in the lines adapted from Suso's *Orologium Sapientiae*, is unabashedly erotic since the allegory insists that the secular equivalent of divine love and attraction is human arousal to sexual stimulation. Wisdom thus speaks of attraction that is on the literal level very physical:

WISDOM

> Beholde now, Sowll, wyth joyfull mynde,
> How louely I am, how amyable,
> To be halsyde and kyssyde of mankynde.
> To all clene sowlys I am full hende
> And euer present wer that they be;
> I loue my lovers wythowtyn ende
> That ther loue haue stedfast in me.
> (ll. 42-48)

The subsequent emphasis on experience and tasting in Wisdom's speech (ll. 50, 63) also points to the physical side of love, which should be totally focused on the figure of the deity who has been revealed through the Incarnation. Anima's response is ecstatic, utilizing words that out of context would seem to be drawn from the secular poetry of love:

> O worthy spowse and soueren fayer,
> O swet amyke, owr joy, owr blys!
> To yowr loue wo dothe repeyer,
> All felycyte yn that creature ys.
> (ll. 69-72)

It will be noted that, even more than the Passion devotion from which this appears to be derived, such a way of understanding the religious experience is very different from the rationalism normally already associated with Dominican theology.[29] Much here depends upon the discovery of a *feeling* within the soul through self-knowledge; as Wisdom explains, "By knowynge of yowrsylff ye may haue felynge/ Wat Gode ys in yowr sowle sensyble" (ll. 95-96). This emotional dimension is not to be underestimated as a force behind the theatrical excitement generated by the play of *Wisdom*.

Even in the design of the costumes, care has been taken to achieve iconographic exactness. Anima's costume at the beginning of the play is indicative of her condition, for she is dressed in white cloth of gold with "a mantyll of blake therwppeon" (*s.d.* at l. 16) to signify the dialectic of fair and foul within the soul. As Wisdom explains to her, the two colors signify

> Yowr dysgysynge and yowr aray,
> Blake and wyght, fowll and fayer vereyly,
> Euery sowll here, this ys no nay,
> Blake by sterynge of synne that cummyth all-day,
> Wyche felynge cummythe of sensualyte,
> Ande wyght by knowenge of reson veray
> Off the blyssyde infenyt Deyte.
>
> Thus a sowle ys bothe fowlle and fayer:
> Fowll as a best be felynge of synne,
> Fayer as an angell, of hewyn the ayer,
> By knowynge of Gode by hys reson wythin.
> (ll. 150-60)

The terms 'fair' and 'foul' will reappear in a much later temptation play, Shakespeare's *Macbeth*,[30] where the words echo the condition of the soul of the hero, who likewise will place this illusory world ahead of a more substantial reality, though Shakespeare's character will in the end fail to repent of his disfiguring deeds. In *Wisdom*, the foulness of sin is presented in terms of feeling just as in *Macbeth*, and this emotional acceptance of evil is set off against knowing through the faculty of reason, which is overwhelmed through deception and the force of evil.

The iconography of *Wisdom* hence implies a value system applied to the visible condition of the soul, Anima. 'Fayre' and 'fowll' are terms which reflect the degree of resemblance between the soul and its Creator--or also between the soul and its chief enemy. Much is made in the play of the idea that the soul has been created in the image and likeness of God. "Wat ys a sowll, wyll ye declare?" asks Anima, and Wisdom answers:

> Yt ys the ymage of Gode that all began;
> And not only ymage, but hys lyknes ye are.
> (ll. 103-04)

These lines are adapted from Hilton's *Scale of Perfection*[31] which carefully distinguishes the state of the soul in terms of how well the divine likeness is preserved. Because of original sin, a new-born child who is as yet not baptized (and who hence is still in original sin) "is nought but an ymage of the fende and a bronde of helle."[32] However, the Sacraments and a proper inward response to the divine realities will restore the soul to fairness. This is the condition of Anima at the beginning of *Wisdom*.

A distinction, nevertheless, needs to be made between image and likeness. For St. John of Damascus,

> Man is created in the image of God. This image is given to him in his spirit and free will. But the image must be revealed in likeness and this is accomplished in freedom and in the gift of the self in love. The likeness to God is realized by effort and sacrifice; it is fulfilled by grace, but not without the freedom of man . . . for the mark of a seal can only be imprinted on wax if it is molten.[33]

As Eugene D. Hill points out, the Western re-interpretation, first by St. Augustine and later by St. Bernard of Clairvaux, of the ideas of *image* and *likeness* in this context is crucial to the use of these terms in *Wisdom*.[34] Augustine had insisted that the image of God in man was an imperfect image which approaches perfection "by a sort of likeness" or similarity: "For approach to God is not by intervals of place, but by likeness, and withdrawal from Him is by unlikeness."[35] For Bernard, the image of God is retained by man, while he may lose his likeness to him.[36] In *Wisdom*, therefore, Anima, the soul, is stamped with God's image: the trinitarian structure of the deity is reflected in the three Mights which make up the faculties of the soul.[37] In this sense the soul is, as Wisdom carefully explains, a "symylytude of Gode abowe" (1. 284). As a baptized soul, Anima also shares a *likeness* with God whom she loves, though in this case the resemblance is not absolute; rather, the likeness is to be compared to the technical achievement of the much admired Flemish paintings which reproduce scenes realistically and yet with meticulous attention to the iconography as a result of a search for verisimilitude in religious pictures--a search which, however, can never produce photographic realism or illustrations that show exactly how the scene originally appeared to those who were actual onlookers in biblical times. The source for the likeness must come from within the individual soul and, because this act involves the soul's freedom, there is also the danger that it may be diverted from the task at hand--and indeed in the play the soul will become disfigured and all too soon will lose its likeness to God.

The problem, implied by the black mantle that Anima wears, lies in the heredity of the race, which is descended from Adam and which hence shares naturally in his Fall. Adam, created in God's image and likeness, can only pass on the image and not the likeness to his descendants. Anima as a soul thus typically inherits the faculties represented by the three Mights--Mind, Will, and Understanding--while she also achieves likeness through her baptism and her subsequent devotion to the Trinity, especially to the Second Person who revealed himself and allowed himself to be sacrificed for all souls. All creatures participate in the "natur of the fyrst man, Adame,/ Off hymn takynge the fylthe of synne orygynall"; hence, "Wen ye be bore fyrst of yowr dame,/ Ye may in no wyse in hewyn dwell,/ For ye be dysvyguryde be hys synne,/ Ande dammyde to derknes from Godys syghte" (ll. 110-11, 115-18). Baptism's function here is to change the soul's condition in a real way by actually cleansing away original sin; in the process, baptism "reformyt the sowll in feythe verray/ To the gloryus lyknes of Gode eternall" (ll. 127-28). Thus are human souls made as perfect and "as fayer and as celestyall/ As yt neuer dyffowlyde had be" so that they might be appropriate resting places or seats for Christ himself (ll. 129-32).

The freedom of the soul suggested as early as St. John of Damascus and reaffirmed in *Wisdom*, however, opens up the possibility that it, fallen from its likeness to the deity, might allow another power, Satan, to occupy it and to tyrannize over it. As Lucifer in the play explains, the soul, which is within man, "ys werely the Deuelys place" when "yt ys in dedly synne" (ll. 545-46). According to the evidence of medieval iconography, the soul ideally should be represented as a well tended garden in which the sweet herbs of virtue will grow and the "wedys of synne" are made "to flee" (ll. 91-92). Unfortunately, the soul can easily become like an unweeded garden--a most significant symbol that, adapted to the body politic, found extensive use as late as Shakespeare. For a useful example from the visual arts we may most conveniently turn to a Flemish painting, since the enclosed garden, shown in weeds and ruin, forms a crucial part of the background for the *Friedsam Annunciation* (Metropolitan Museum of Art)[38] where it illustrates the corrupting influence of the world of promiscuous growth and decay--a world that is set off against the permanence of the building which represents the religion revealed in the Old and New Testaments.[39] So too the soul, corrupted by its contact with the world, may allow itself to grow up as if in choking weeds at the same time that its purpose and function are allowed to fall to ruin. This will in a sense happen in the course of the theatrical action of the Macro *Wisdom* as orderly behavior is exchanged for unruly dancing and for music which stands in opposition to the beauty of liturgical chant, the preferred music of the monastic tradition. In this instance, the iconography is symbolically if not literally visible through the stage spectacle which is adopted.

When examined superficially and without reference to the theatrical effectiveness of the drama, Anima seems to be undramatically passive, lacking control over her fate rather than representing any of the freedom normally accorded to the soul. "Anima is a puppet who suffers rather than acts," Eccles complains.[40] Spivack argues more broadly that the usual figure of mankind in the moralities is here "not a personification but a universalized type; and he is placed in the position, absurd from the viewpoint of allegory, of fraternizing with his personified attributes."[41] Concerning the mankind figure in Medwall's *Nature*, he adds: "Man stands by a mute listener while his Sensuality and his Reason argue their separate claims to dominion over him, until finally he bursts out like a wonder-stricken and utterly forlorn third party. . . ."[42] As Natalie Crohn Schmitt has argued, however, the reaction of the "third party" is indeed upon reflection consistent with our experience even today; phenomenologically, we still separate our emotions and faculties from ourselves upon occasion, as when we say, "A wave of joy swept over me" or "I have lost my mind."[43] The Mind, Will, or Understanding--or even the five senses--are not absolutely identified with the person, but *belong* to him or her.[44] Nevertheless, in *Wisdom* the Three Mights and the various inward and outward senses represent Anima's freedom, for they are her means of obtaining information about reality or the world and of processing that information. They are the means also by which temptation can come to her. At the same time, the three Mights at least are essential to her reform at the end of the play.

In the drama, the spectacle of the processional entrance of the five inward senses or "wyttys of my sowll wythinne" (l. 163) is placed prior to the speeches of the three Mights, and they leave together in procession at the end of the scene when the stage is to be entirely cleared in preparation for the entry of Lucifer at line 325. If the "wyttys" were merely the five outward senses which are gateways to this world, it would be most strange that Anima should refer to them as "fyve prudent vyrgyns" (l. 162).[45] And when they appear they are dressed in white kirtles and mantles with wigs and chaplets, the head covering also worn by Anima though hers is described as "ryche" and "lasyde behynde hangynge down wyth t[w]o knottys of golde and syde tasselys" (*s.d.* at l. 16). As they enter, the five wits sing an antiphon, "Nigra sum sed formosa, filia Jerusalem," that takes its text from the *Song of Songs* 1.4. The virgins are, as noted above, the five prudent ones ("quinque prudentes," l. 173), surely to be identified also with the five wise virgins ("prudentes," in the Vulgate rendering) from the parable of the Wise and Foolish Virgins.[46] As the inward senses, they are to be properly watchful, in contrast to the five outward senses of sight, hearing, taste, smell, and touch which were commonly identified with the five foolish virgins.[47] "Kepe yow clene and ye xall neuer deface," Wisdom advises the inward wits (l. 174). When they sing again as they go out, they will intone another antiphon, "Tota pulcra es," presumably "Tota pulchra es amica" which is one of the processional antiphons for Trinity Sunday in the Sarum Missal.[48] Again the text is from the *Song of Songs*, which would hardly be appropriate for the five outward senses.

At the end of the play, Anima confesses that she has offended in both her "inwarde wyttys" or spiritual senses and her "outwarde wyttys" or "fyve wyttys bodyly" (ll. 1074-76). The latter were considered to be psychologically the more dangerous to the well-being of the soul. In *Jacob's Well*, they are described as gateways that require to be stopped up if the soul is to be kept from corruption.[49] Representations of these bodily senses are conveniently but emblematically included in the wall painting above the fireplace on the east wall at Longthorpe Tower.[50] At the end of each of the five spokes of a Wheel of the Senses are symbols signifying sight (a cock), taste (a monkey), smell (a vulture), touch (a spider), and hearing (a boar). At the center of the wheel of the senses is a man, crowned and wearing a mantle over his tunic; his left hand is placed on the spoke which terminates in the symbol for hearing. This iconography may be compared with the Wheel of Life in the De Lisle Psalter (fol. 126v; fig. 19), for in the manuscript illumination the head of the deity appears at the wheel's hub.[51] In the one wheel, man is at the center, while in the other God is at the center. In the one case, the senses serve man, while in the other all acts of one's life are properly subordinated to the order of the creation and its Creator. The Wheel of the Senses thus would seem to illustrate the self-love that St. Augustine compared with holy love, which in contrast is directed outward toward neighbor and deity rather than toward the self.[52]

In *Wisdom*, Anima recites extensive reasons for following holy love, for she is bound to God in numerous ways (ll. 309-22). Not without significance, the list of benefits concludes with the anointing of the soul with the "oyll of mercy" (l. 321), which would seem to refer to the chrism used since the early Church in the rite of baptism. However, though not literalized in *Wisdom*, the traditional iconography of the Oil of Mercy is significant for our understanding of the theological and devotional structure of the play. The presence of the Oil of Mercy establishes an echo apparently designed to remind the audience of the oil which Adam at his death asked his son Seth to search out from the angel at the gate of Eden.[53] Instead, the angel gave him three seeds from the apple eaten by Adam at the Fall. In painted glass at St. Neots, Cornwall, Seth's vision of a great tree in the garden of Eden which reaches from hell up to heaven and which holds the Christ Child in its branches appears as background, while in the foreground he places the three seeds under his father's tongue as he lies on his deathbed.[54] When these seeds have grown from Adam's grave, they will have produced the wood to be used in the cross of the Crucifixion. According to the legend, Christ himself will be the

Oil of Mercy offered to all who are baptized and who will live the vigilant life. This legend, then, provides a context for understanding the reference to the oil in line 321.

The psychology of the vigilant life--a life necessary if one is to achieve the benefits of mystical experience--is more complex than might at first be imagined, particularly if the context is that of Benedictine monasticism. The moral landscape was then the object of considerable concern, and the subtleties of analysis in a play such as *Wisdom* would appear to exceed modern writings in exactitude on the very basic questions that are raised. The five spiritual senses, to be sure, overlap with the figures of Mind, Will, and Understanding, and yet both the senses and the Mights remain separate in the play. In order to avoid confusion, the inward or "fyve wyttys of [the] sowll wythinne" are not individually named in the play, while every effort is made to distinguish clearly between the three Mights and these senses. Thus, while the three Mights share the color white with the five spiritual senses, the former are nevertheless very carefully set apart visually by their livery, which appropriately identifies them as servants of the soul. Furthermore, careful visual distinctions are retained in the procession which empties the playing area at the end of the first scene; here the five wits are the ones who sing the antiphon as they are "goyng befor" Anima, who in turn is followed by the three Mights.

The Three Mights, which reflect the image of the Trinity in man,[55] are carefully warned by Wisdom to be on their guard against the Three Enemies of Man. Mind, which is associated with *faith*, is at first very aware of his weakness and his need to rely on God's stability. "I seke and fynde nowere comforte/ But only in Gode, my Creator," he insists (ll. 205-06). He will be most weak, however, when faced with the *suggestions* of the *devil*--i.e., with the beginning of sinful acts. Understanding, whose psychological function is not fully distinguished from Mind in the drama,[56] nevertheless is set apart by his association with *hope* and by his susceptibility at the second stage of temptation, *delight*, wherein, as might be expected if contemplative monasticism is the ideal from which the soul is falling away, the *world* will play a principal role in the corrupting of this faculty. Finally, Will, whose rightful attachment is to love or *charity*, not surprisingly moves the soul toward the final stage in temptation, *consent*, while his own corruption comes principally through the *flesh*. Wisdom thus warns:

> Wan suggestyon to the Mynde doth apere,
> Wndyrstondynge, delyght not ye therin;
> Consent not, Wyll, yll lessons to lere,
> Ande than suche sterynges be no syn.
> (ll. 301-04)

But the devil, the world, and the flesh will have their day, and in the next scene the process of temptation will begin successfully to separate the Mights from faith, hope, and charity.

Lucifer in his own form enters the playing area in the second scene of *Wisdom*. He is distorted and ugly beyond belief as he announces his plan to work his wiles upon the soul of mankind. Once he had been the most beautiful angel in heaven, but now he is appropriately most repulsive in appearance since he is "lowest in hell" (l. 336). He is extremely hostile to mankind, toward whom he shows great malice and envy. Hence his object will be to disfigure man's soul which is as yet the "fygure" of the deity and "Hys symylytude, hys pyctowre,/ Gloryosest of ony creature/ That euer was wrought" (ll. 349-52). His plan as revealed to the audience in his soliloquy is precisely that which Wisdom had warned against in the previous scene:

> To the Mynde of the Soule I xall mak suggestyun,
> Ande brynge hys Wndyrstondynge to dylectacyon,
> So that hys Wyll make confyrmacyon;
>   Than am I sekyr inowe
> That dethe xall sew of damnacyon;
> Than of the Sowll the Dewell hath dominacyon.
> (ll. 365-70)

Of course, in his own form the devil will hardly succeed in loosening Mind's resolve to remain in the faith; thus he will "change me into bryhtnes,/ And so hym to-begyle" (ll. 375-76). The stage direction that appears at Lucifer's initial entry explains the costume that he will be wearing: "entreth LUCYFER in a dewellys aray wythowt[,] and wythin as a prowde galonte." His change to the costume and form of a gallant takes place offstage, as the next stage direction (following l. 380) indicates: "Her LUCYFER dewoydyth and cummyth in ageyn as a goodly galont." This trick of the devil will look forward to a similar offstage change by a devil, Mephostophilis' transformation in Marlowe's *Doctor Faustus* from "ugly" to the "shape" of "an old Franciscan friar" ("That holy shape becomes a devil best," Faustus says) (iii.25-28).[57]

Lucifer's assault on Mind and the other Mights begins with a biblical quotation (from *Matthew* 20.6) that accuses them of idleness through the deliberate confusion of their contemplative stance with inactivity. Iconographically, the temptation of Mind, who begins by arguing against the twisted statements of Lucifer, repeats in some sense the temptation of Adam and Eve in the Garden of Eden, for at the beginning of history the devil was believed also to have come to mankind in a false shape and to have used sophistry, at that time encouraging the eating of the apple which would be an emblem of pride and gluttony--i.e., an indulging of both the spirit and the body. In *Wisdom*, Lucifer's attack appears to be directed against the *mixed life* encouraged by the late medieval mystics,[58] though his arguments seem actually to involve an attempt to discredit the contemplative life in favor of the active life--an active life that, however, he defines in terms of worldly activity without a spiritual dimension. This will be a life exactly opposed to the Benedictine ideal. Rather curiously, Lucifer's version of the mixed life would provide no challenge to the spirit at all, and his final admonition before Mind weakens suggests that it is better not to strive too hard to rise toward spiritual perfection since that way lies only despair. "Who clymyt hye, hys fall gret ys," he concludes (l. 444), falling back on a proverb.[59] The demonic plea to Mind suggests something which superficially seems precisely opposed to the devil's "you shall be as Gods" spoken to Eve in *Genesis* 3.5, and yet ultimately the result of the temptation will be to return the soul to the same condition that Eve and Adam had achieved by their trespass. In *Wisdom*, however, that state of trespass is emblemized by the disfigurement of the soul, Anima, whose appearance will in fact be shocking when she reappears in the acting area.

Now Lucifer will encourage "Yowr fyve wyttys abrode [to] lett sprede" (l. 453) in order to allow Understanding to have contact with the temptations of the world, to which he will respond by announcing his feeling of "dylectacyon" (l. 462). Will likewise is affected by the five senses, who "gyff informacyon" seemingly indicating that Lucifer's "resons be goode" (ll. 479-80). The process of letting the five wits gather "informacyon" is not visualized but reported. Nevertheless, the result is disastrous to the soul, who will receive an unacceptable degree of corruption through the gateways of the five senses. While the freedom possessed by the soul's faculties has brought them to this, Lucifer is of course arguing falsely when he suggests that the "Wyll of the Soule hathe fre dominacyon" even over reason (l. 481). Paradoxically, Will, by submitting himself to the tyranny of the flesh, will lose his freedom until such time that he will reclaim his lost innocence. Quoting a proverb, Will says, "Ya, I woll no more row ageyn the floode" (l. 491).

While the three Mights will lose their freedom in their new-found life of sinfulness and crime, their transformation also will largely cause them to lose their identities. At one level they become representatives of Pride, Covetousness, and Lechery, but these are given more than abstract representation in the play, which sets them forth as Maintenance, Bribery (or Perjury), and Lust. Mind, Understanding, and Will thus become the social abuses to which they have fallen.[60] Having changed their costumes, they now appear in new disguise as insufferable gallants who not only come together to sing a song (presumably bawdy, though the text and tune are not given), but also to act in ways that are coordinated to seem most insufferable. Revelling and cheating and whoring in the region of London and its suburbs, the three Mights in fact forget who they are.

In the arrangement of dramatic material--material that is formalized and somewhat ritualized--each of the Mights is joined by six other figures in a dance. The first to be thus joined by other dancers is Mind, whose partners in the dance have red beards and wear his livery. Each has a staff in his hand. Between them, they will represent the sins of the devil--i.e., Pride, Wrath, and Envy--

though their names are Indignation, Sturdiness (i.e., Stubbornness), Malice, Hastiness, Wreche (i.e., Vengeance), and Discord, with Mind making up the seventh whose name is Maintenance. "Seven ys a numbyr of dyscorde and inperfyghtnes," says Mind (l. 697). With a trumpet played by the minstrels, the tableau is complete. The musical instrument that is used is iconographically correct, for it is the instrument of pride. Associated with royalty, the trumpet was intended to impress spectators with its sound in pageantry and in military usage. Even the trumpeters were often accorded special status as musicians. But ironically the trumpet, or at least a horn shaped like this instrument, was one that was commonly placed in the hands of demons in and around hell;[61] the use of the mouthpiece and the manner of making sounds amplified in the trumpet had scatological associations in the later Middle Ages. Quite appropriately, therefore, Mind announces the dance to be danced as "the Deullys dance" (l. 700). With seven participants, we may assume that this dance was a round dance which moved from right to left (i.e., counterclockwise). In the Middle Ages, such dances were frequently danced in the churchyard on the north (or devil's) side of the church, and they were often frowned upon by the clergy. According to one critic, "a ring-dance is a circle at whose centre is the devil, and everyone is turning perversely [*ad sinistrum*]."[62] Yet, as Mind indicates in the play, there is a further level of irony in the music that accompanies the dance, for trumpets were also regarded as the instruments that "xulde blow to the jugemente" (l. 702) at the last day of history.

The second set of dancers are dressed as jurors "in a sute, gownyde, wyth hodys abowt her nekys, hattys of meyntenance thervpon, vyseryde dyuersly" (*s.d.* after l. 724). In this case, the six dancers are Wrong, Sleight, Doubleness, Falseness, Raveyn (i.e., Robbery), and Deceit, who are of course joined by the seventh, Understanding, who is now transformed to Perjury, designed to feed his covetousness. The music for the dance is provided by a single minstrel with a bagpipe, an instrument commonly associated with popular dancing, and indeed Understanding comments that these dancers "daunce all the londe hydyr and thedyr" (l. 732).

Will, as the leader of the third group of dancers, together with them will sum up the sins of the Flesh, which are Gluttony, Lechery, and Sloth. Specifically, the six dancers who join him are women, with three of them disguised as gallants and three as "matrones"; all wear masks. Their names are Rekleshede (i.e., Heedlessness), Idleness, Surfeit-and-Greediness, Spousebreach, Mistress, and Fornication, to which Will adds Lust or Lechery. Again a minstrel plays for the dance, this time with a hornpipe, which is an obvious symbol of the cuckold since it "fowll ys in hymselff but to the erys swete" (l. 758).[63] Will has promised that the dance will be a spectacle confusing truth and lying (with a pun intended in the term 'lying'); "Ye xall se a sprynge of Lechery," he has assured his companions (l. 747). Quite clearly the dance is so impudent that even Mind is offended, and a quarrel begins. In iconography, the dance has a traditional association with the sins of the Flesh, and hence when Mary Magdalene is shown falling into such sins in the Digby *Mary Magdalene* and in an etching by Lucas van Leyden,[64] she dances with a lover in surroundings that typify the pleasures that come from indulging the body.

The state of things as dramatized in this scene in *Wisdom* cannot continue indefinitely. Mind and Understanding want to pursue the *gaining* of worldly prestige and of wealth, while Will focuses his attention on whoring and *spending*.[65] All of these pursuits are, however, represented as intellectually shallow, emotionally unsatisfying, and spiritually debilitating--quite the antithesis of the kind of life recommended by the mystics of the late Middle Ages. What is worse, the three Mights do not seem to realize what has happened to them. They are indeed so alienated from the stability of the deity that they find themselves totally lost in this unstable world--so totally lost that they do not even recognize their condition for what it is. The intent of the play at this point is to show that all their merriment is hollow, and this is effected visually. What will be required to return them to their former condition will be the sight of Wisdom, the image of Christ, who will remind them of realities higher than the mere titillation they have been receiving from their secular activities.

Wisdom speaks to Mind as the messenger of revealed truth:

O thou Mynde, remembyr the!

WISDOM

> Turne thi weys, thou gost amyse.
> Se what thi ende ys, thou myght not fle:
> Dethe to euery creature certen ys.
> They that lyue well, they xall haue blys;
> Thay that endyn yll, they goo to hell.
> I am Wysdom, sent to tell yow thys:
> Se in what stat thou doyst indwell.
> (ll. 873-80)

The play of *Wisdom*, therefore, is intended to function as an extended visual reminder of man's earthly fate according to contemporary theology and hence of the Ash Wednesday liturgy, which sets out to bring to a person's remembrance the thought that mankind was created of dust and to dust he shall return. This belief was indeed regarded as the ultimate fact of human existence against which one's life may be tested.[66] Not surprisingly, Mind, who thinks he has been having fun, tries to deny the immediacy of what Wisdom is saying. This kind of denial is best examined through the iconography of the Dance of Death which illustrates the reluctance with which most persons meet Death. Though Mind is being called to life instead of death, thus also does he beg Wisdom for more time: "We may amende wen we be sage" (l. 892). Such a request for more time, which would seem to have a possible source in St. Augustine's plea of "Not yet, O Lord" in his *Confessions*, appears also as a commonplace in the Middle English lyric:

> Louerd, thu clepedest me
> An ich nagt ne ansuarede the
> Bute wordes scloe and sclepie:
> "thole yet! thole a litel!"
> But "yiet" and "yiet" was endelis,
> And "thole a litel" a long wey is.[67]

Wisdom thus complains about those who continue to "slumber and wynke" when called to account: "They take not drede before ther face,/ Howe horryble ther synnys stynke" (ll. 894-96). Nevertheless, the soul in this instance is ultimately not one of the incorrigible ones metaphorically described in the Rule of St.

Benedict as hopelessly diseased.[68]

Reality appears to break through for Mind when Wisdom calls forth Anima, whose form is entirely disfigured. For Mind, the shock of recognition is very great indeed: he is afraid and trembles since the soul is "fowler than ony fende" (l. 904). The deadly sins which Mind, Will, and Understanding have used are now literally infecting Anima: "As many dedly synnys as ye haue vsyde,/ So many deullys in yowr soule be" (ll. 909-10). When Wisdom calls attention to the demons, seven boys[69] representing small devils run from under the mantle of Anima and then run back under it again. The iconography here is clearly related to the story of Mary Magdalene as understood in the Middle Ages and as dramatized in the Digby play, for this composite figure, who is known in scholarship as the "single Magdalene," was held to be the woman from whom Christ expelled the seven demons commonly believed by medieval commentators to be the Seven Deadly Sins.[70] But Anima is additionally made to seem very ugly, worse in appearance than a demon. The source of this iconographic detail might also be St. Augustine, who had insisted in the *City of God*, Book XIV, 4, that "When, therefore, man lives according to man, not according to God, he is like the devil."[71] In any case, the likeness of God is here changed to a flaming torch out of hell (ll. 917-18). The physical transformation reflects the change in Anima's spiritual condition and also illustrates the way in which this drama utilizes visual statement to probe the soul's inner condition.

The stages by which the Mights are restored to their original state are now explored in the play. The first stage illustrates the recognition by the Mights that they have gone awry in their behavior and attitude. An impetus which motivates their movement toward reform will be the depression and despair of Anima. Despair is again a dramatically appropriate attitude in this case, since it was regarded as sometimes necessary for the reformation of the soul.[72] All four--the three Mights or faculties as well as the entire soul itself--cry out for mercy. They are not yet ready, however, for the forgiveness of sins which will be the final stage in the process that is underway.

Contrition is required, for this quality is the "purger and clenser of synne" (l. 962). Especially useful in this process will be a small visual device, a tear shed with sorrow "That rubbyt and waschyt the Soule wythin" (l. 964). As we might expect from our knowledge of the Northern spirituality of this period, the tears shed by Anima are crucial. When she weeps, she begins to awaken from her spiritual slumber, and out from under her mantle come the boys impersonating the demons who are the Seven Deadly Sins. The iconography of the play illustrates the effectiveness of the soul's contrition; as Wisdom explains, "Lo, how contrycyon avoydyth the deullys blake!/ Dedly synne ys non yow wythin" (ll. 979-80). However, though she no longer harbors deadly sin, her appearance illustrates that the task of re-forming herself is but half done. Anima must participate in the Sacrament of Confession before she can have her "charter of pardon" (l. 986), which can be given to her only by "Holy Chyrch." Forgiveness will be required before she can be restored to her previous form. As she prepares to go out to confess to the Church, a commonly-represented allegorical figure who does not appear in the playing area, she prays:

> O Fadyr of mercy ande of comfort,
>   Wyth wepynge ey and hert contryte
> To owr modyr, Holy Chyrche, I wyll resort,
>   My lyff pleyn schewenge to here syght.
> Wyth Mynde, Vndyrstondynge, and Wyll ryght,
>   Wyche of my Sowll the partyes be,
> To the domys of the Chyrche we xall vs dyght,
>   Wyth veray contricyon thus compleynnyng we.
>   (ll. 989-96)

As she goes out in procession with Mind, Will, and Understanding, she sings "in the most lamentabull wyse, wyth drawte notys as yt ys songyn in the passyon wyke"; the words of her lament are from the *Lamentations* of Jeremiah 2.13 and 1.2. Father Molloy notes that these verses were chanted on Holy Thursday at Matins and also suggests that the procession of the soul and the Three Mights may have been modelled on the procession of penitents on this day in cathedral churches.[73] The text of the verses from *Lamentations*, however, is significant here in its own right, for identification of the soul in this context with the sorrowful city of Jerusalem is quite accurate: the earthly Jerusalem, normally recognized as the

Church, is the community of believers who look forward eventually to a higher existence in the heavenly Jerusalem. According to the *Apocalypse*, the Church or New Jerusalem, which has its source in heaven, has been "prepared as a bride adorned for her husband" (21.2). The Holy Week emphasis additionally serves as a reminder that hope of reform and transformation is only possible through suffering, for Christ himself had to endure his Passion in order for the Sacraments of the Church to be established.

In *Wisdom*, Anima's confession before Holy Church is not shown since it takes place off stage while Wisdom recites in didactic fashion the nine points which will please God most.[74] The off-stage Church, who is a Virgin and a Mother, is at once identified also as the Body of Christ (i.e., those who live in hope of salvation in this world) and as the institution or Church hierarchy in history. Because she shows Christ to the world through the Sacraments, especially through the power of the keys evidenced in Penance and in the Eucharist--i.e., the power given to St. Peter and his followers to release men and women from the tyranny of sin when Christ made his gift of "the keys of the kingdom of heaven" (*Matt.* 16.19) to him--Mother Church is the window through which the Incarnation is revealed to men and women. The Church is also the source of their spiritual rebirth. But as the Body of Christ, she is additionally the Spouse (*Sponsa*) of Christ, who is the Bridegroom (*Sponsus*).[75]

In the visual arts, the Church (*Ecclesia*) is most commonly represented in contrast with the Synagogue; whereas the one sees with the eyes of faith and hopes for a more direct experience of spiritual love, the other is symbolically blindfolded, while her broken staff illustrates the weakness of her support. Unlike Ecclesia, Synagoga has lost her way in the world, and her crown is falling from her head. Such details are to be found in numerous examples in English art beginning at least as early as the twelfth century, as in examples on the Norman font (fig. 20) at Southrop in Gloucestershire (c.1160),[76] on the late thirteenth-century painted ceiling formerly in the Chapter House at York Minster as well as in painted glass in the Chapter House vestibule from approximately the same date,[77] and in an illuminated initial in the Huth Psalter (British Library Add. MS. 38,116), fol. 119^v, from 1280-1300.[78]

Frequently Ecclesia holds a cross and a church, as in painted glass at York, where the church may suggest identification with the hierarchy. Ecclesia's crown is the biblical "crown of life" (*James* 1.12, *Apocalypse* 2.10), but it is also related to the crown that is awarded to the Blessed Virgin in the popular Coronation of the Virgin scenes, which in turn owe much to the earlier iconography of the Church as *Sponsa* being greeted by the *Sponsus*. The connection between the allegorical Ecclesia and the Mother of God is thus, to be sure, quite close in iconography. For the later Middle Ages, this point is perhaps best illustrated by means of a continental example, a Flemish painting. Jan van Eyck's *Madonna in a Church* shows the Blessed Virgin, crowned and much larger than in life, holding her Child and standing in the nave of a Gothic church while in the choir a service is in progress.[79] Here the Virgin is also Ecclesia, "the bride and mother of the Bridegroom."[80]

After receiving absolution off-stage from Holy Church, Anima is crowned and restored to her original beauty with her former garments, while the five wits and three Mights are likewise restored and crowned. These are the crowns promised by Wisdom earlier in the play (l. 307) and are iconographically identical with the crown of life traditionally worn by Ecclesia, who is to be sure not described in the play. The procession at this point is, however, carefully described:

> Here entrethe ANIMA, wyth the Fyve Wyttys goynge before, MYNDE on the on syde and WNDYRSTONDYNGE on the other syde and WYLL folowyng, all in here fyrst clothynge, her chapplettys and crestys, . . . syngynge in here commynge in: 'Quid retribuam Domino pro omnibus que retribuit mihi? Calicem salutaris accipiam et nomen Domini inuocabo.' (*s.d.* following l. 1064)

The antiphon which they sing is derived from Psalm 115 (116): "What shall I render to the Lord, for all the things that he hath rendered to me? I will take up the chalice of salvation; and I will call upon the name of the Lord" (vv. 12-13). The "chalice of salvation" refers in the medieval reading of the psalm text to the Eucharist specifically, and hence Father Molloy plausibly suggests that Anima may also have received Communion in addition to absolution.[81] In any event, what has happened has successfully washed away the ugly and demonic disfiguration that Anima has sustained. In a sense, the result is the same as that which is illustrated in a Seven Sacraments font at Westhall, Suffolk, where a man kneels on a pillow and receives absolution from a priest; beside the man is the figure of his guardian angel, while behind him is the devil, who is turned away with his tail literally between his legs (fig. 21).[82] Therefore, through her experience of the Sacraments, Anima has been cleansed by Christ's Passion and has been given "a new resurreccyon" (l. 1071) that has driven away the power of the devil, who has been defeated by the higher power inherent in the rites of the Church. The effect of it all has been to make the soul and her constituent parts--i.e., the wits and the three Mights--worthy of the "crownnys victoryall/ To regne in blys wythowtyn ende" (ll. 1115-16).

Anima is reformed on the level of her *feelings* and also her *reason*, and she has been restored to God's *likeness*. The "old man" of whom St. Paul speaks (*Ephesians* 4.22) must be given up, and this is possible only because of the atonement. Thus can the soul be renewed in grace and reunited with the source of all goodness within the created universe:

> Now wyth Sent Powle we may sey thus
> That be reformyde thorow feythe in Jhesum:
> We haue peas and acorde betwyx Gode and ws.
> (ll. 1148-50)

The allegory comes to its ending in the play of *Wisdom*, as in *Mankind*, with the representative human soul reconciled and the principles of mercy sustained. Such a happy conclusion in the morality genre seems to be the norm, to be sure, until the Protestant era when W. Wager, in a play like *Enough Is As Good As a Feast* (c.1570), would consign his protagonist, Worldly Man, to the place of damnation. In *Wisdom* the soul, however, is reformed as she is returned to the likeness of the deity, and the return to this likeness once more impels the soul and the faculties of Mind, Will, and Understanding toward what was considered a proper devotional and mystical stance in relation to the character of Wisdom, who provides the central image around which the action of the play is arranged.

In the conclusion, as we have seen above, Wisdom appears as a figure like the devotional images illustrating Christ in the late Middle Ages--images which make much of the wounds in hands, feet, and heart as well as of the marks of the Scourging which cover him from his head to his toes, and which thus show his "body full of holys, as a dovehows" (l. 1106). This comparison in particular is one that is taken directly from English and continental mystical literature,[83] and was sufficiently commonplace to be drawn upon by Margery Kempe in her description of her vision of the Savior on the Cross as "alto-rent and toryn wyth scorgys, mor ful of wowndys than euyr was duffehows of holys. . . ."[84] Concerning the use of this metaphor by the English mystics, Wolfgang Riehle has commented: "It would be wrong to dismiss such an image as a lapse in good taste, for it is precisely in a metaphor which seems to be so far-fetched that the focal point is not the sensual idea but the spiritual content it conveys, in this case the concept that Christ with his wounds has become a place of refuge not just for the individual soul but for all mankind."[85] Such likewise is intended to be the lesson of *Wisdom*, which sets out to promote the understanding of the Christian experience not merely in terms of theatrical repetition of the Fall and recovery but also as response to the suffering Christ made visible through his image displayed for all Christians to see. Hence if the figure of Wisdom in the play reminds us at first of the Christ in Majesty, close examination of this figure especially in the latter part of the play will suggest that the Second Person of the Trinity is actually to be visualized in a strongly emotional manner consistent with the English mystical tradition of the late Middle Ages.

The working out of the action of the play is similarly dependent on visual transformations, on the polarities between which man's soul gravitates, and on the balanced theatrical tableaux which are the result of a symmetrical dramatic structure. It is a drama which invites the audience to join imaginatively in the events which occur and to participate in the devotional stance that is encouraged throughout. At the ending of the play, the contemplative life is reaffirmed, and the mystical endeavor as well as its relation to image theology are authenticated.

IV

LIFE'S TERMINUS AND THE MORALITY DRAMA

It will be apparent from the analyses of the plays of the Macro manuscript in the previous chapters that both the iconography literalized in the dramas--i.e., made visible as part of the "stage picture"--and the iconographic context that otherwise informs this drama need to be studied together in order to understand these survivals of the fifteenth-century theater. In either case, iconography is the result of visual and spatial imagination, whether that imagination as displayed in the dramas is immediately theatrical or an invoking of a context which exists outside what is literally seen on the stage. The result is always the careful definition of visual concepts, which are concrete rather than abstract because they are rooted in the sense of sight. Spectacle on the stage and in its iconographic context is essentially linked to the way in which human existence was perceived in the pre-Reformation period. Further, this treatment in the theater of human existence is capable of being understood more clearly in its phenomenological basis by examination of the manner in which the critical issue of the end of life as understood during this period became the groundwork for knowledge about the significance of life with its inevitable moral and psychological conflicts.

On the stage and within the iconographic context as expressed or made visible elsewhere--i.e., in the visual arts, ranging, for example, from humble wall paintings to aristocratic illuminated manuscripts--the collective imagination of the time seems to have turned with surprising frequency to depictions of Death, which was personified as a grisly and unwelcome guest. Without the concerns raised by an awareness of the terminus of life, however, it is certain that the morality drama as it appears in the extant examples in the Macro manuscript would not have been written or staged. Nor, indeed, would we have *Everyman*--a play translated and adapted from Dutch and yet the best-known of the English moralities--to which useful reference will also be made in this chapter.

In examining the context of fifteenth-century concern with man's fragility and ultimately with his mortality, we may begin with an illuminating statement by the allegorical character Reason in Henry Medwall's Nature, Part II, which insists that man abides "wythin the garyson/ Of the frayll carcas and carynouse body," striving always to fend off the attacks of the Three Enemies of Man.[1] The fifteenth century represents a time when people thought of themselves as even more susceptible to disease and death than had been the case prior to the fourteenth century, when the period of demographic expansion came to a halt across Europe and attitudes and modes of religiosity began to be transformed.[2] By the late fourteenth century, therefore, there was a new earnestness about things spiritual as these touched the lives of lay people, whose participation in auricular confession had now become obligatory under the rules of the Church.[3] A new emphasis was placed also on teaching and didacticism, and in a very real sense this effort was the practical result of earlier reforms designed to produce laymen better educated in spiritual matters.[4] One of the effects of these changes in emphasis was to produce a strain of mysticism that may easily be charted in such English writers as Richard Rolle, Julian of Norwich, and even the eccentric Margery Kempe. This mysticism, which helped to establish the intellectual matrix out of which, as we have seen, the play of *Wisdom* in the Macro manuscript arose, was on the whole quite consistent with the thrust of popular religion in England from the fourteenth century until the Reformation, for the heart of the matter was a realization of how close men and women are to a life which exists beyond the life of the body.

In his classic book on background to Elizabethan drama, Willard Farnham quotes St. Thomas More's *Four Last Things*, an unfinished meditation written about 1522:

LIFE'S TERMINUS

> For nothyng is there that maye more effectuallye withdrawe the soule fro the wretched affections of the body, than may the remembrance of death, yf we do not remember it houerly [i.e., inattentively], as one heareth a worde, and let it passe by hys eare, without any receiuing of the sentence into his heart. But if we not onely here this word death, but also let sink into our heartes, the very fantasye and depe imaginacion therof, we shall parceiue therby, that we wer neuer so gretly moued by the beholding of the dance of death pictured in Poules, as we shall fele our self stered and altered, by the feling of that imaginacion in our hertes.[5]

To the "dance of death pictured in Poules" we shall return shortly, but for the moment it is important to understand how frighteningly close to the other world life then seemed to be. More's statement here precisely catches the dominant attitude of thoughtful men in the late medieval period--a period that meditated on suffering, death, and mortality to a degree that has genuinely offended many modern critics, caught up as they have been in the modern repugnance toward such subjects.

More's emphasis on life's terminus--an emphasis that is crucial to our response to the Macro plays as well as to other pre-Reformation moralities, including, of course, the well-known *Everyman*--is derived directly from medieval traditions of popular theology, which were especially expressed through sermons and treatises in the vernacular.[6] This focus has been described by G. R. Owst[7] and on the whole is a commonly noticed characteristic of late medieval spirituality, especially in Northern Europe. As Huizinga notes in his *Waning of the Middle Ages*, "No other epoch has laid so much stress as the expiring of the Middle Ages on the thought of death. An everlasting call of *memento mori* resounds through life."[8] Death in this period quite naturally finds expression most forcefully in the visual arts. Following Émile Mâle's work on late medieval art earlier in the twentieth century, it was the fashion among many art historians to deplore the excessive obsession with death among the artists of the fifteenth century, who were regarded by such scholars as somehow decadent or even perverse.[9] Yet, the theme of death as commonly illustrated in the visual arts likewise had become an essential ingredient in drama prior to the writing of the great tragedies of the Renaissance stage which in their own way also drew upon the remnants of this fascination with life's terminus. Here we must return to a question that has been held over from Chapter II of this study. Specifically, we need at this point to document the relationship between the iconography of death in art and the spectacle of one of the Macro moralities, *The Castle of Perseverance*.

Death, identified in the text of *The Castle of Perseverance* in the Macro manuscript as Mors, is a personification who, literally carrying his mortal dart, comes onto the stage at line 2778 and speaks 65 lines before he gives Humanum Genus a deadly stroke which pierces the man's heart to the "rote."[10] Because the protagonist is hardly ready for his end, the Death who comes into the acting area or platea is no sign of comfort or solace, but is even called "*drery* Dethe" (l. 2790; italics mine). Through death, all are brought to nothing, though they may be great lords and ladies in the land. Even the most handsomely dressed persons will at last be caught in his shroud. Thus Death announces himself as the great leveller, for he brings to a common end everyone alive whether "Ryche, pore, fre and bonde;/ Whanne I come thei goo no more" (ll. 2798-99). All dread his "launce," for, he says quite accurately, "Ageyns me is no defens" (ll. 2807, 2814).

As if to underline the point about his great power, Death invokes a relatively recent catastrophe: "In the grete pestelens/ Thanne was I wel knowe" (ll. 2815-16). The reference here seems to be to the events of 1348-49, when the bubonic plague ravaged the population of England and indeed of all Europe, but it should be recalled that there also were subsequent major outbreaks of the plague in 1360-61, 1369, and 1374 as well as several instances in the early fifteenth century.[11] The onslaught of the bubonic plague, which arrived first in England through Melcombe on the Dorset coast and Southampton, had an effect that is hard to gauge today. Villages were decimated, towns and cities substantially reduced in size, and entire institutions laid waste. The most vivid description of the plague is still Boccaccio's in the Introduction to the *Decameron*, and though he is detailing events in Italy we can be sure that they apply equally to England:

LIFE'S TERMINUS

It started in the East, either because of the influence of heavenly bodies or because of God's just wrath as a punishment to mortals for our wicked deeds, and it killed an infinite number of people. Without pause it spread from one place and it stretched its miserable length over the West. And against this pestilence no human wisdom or foresight was of any avail....[12]

At Ashwell, Hertfordshire, a Latin graffito dated 1350 describes the calamity: "wretched, fierce, violent . . . the dregs of the populace live to tell the tale."[13] A second outbreak of the plague is also recorded in this same graffito. An example of continental iconography, a plague banner from Italy, presents the terror of the plague by means of the threatening figure of Death (here represented with bat-like wings), whose darts have suddenly become more terrible through the instrumentality of the feared disease, though in this case the Blessed Virgin gives protection to the frightened souls while the angels likewise take up their cause.[14] All the other comforts of life which might insulate one from the threats of death have been dissolved, and the immediacy of death confronted every man and woman. Who could tell, therefore, when the healthiest and strongest might face their mortality?

But Humanum Genus is hardly at his healthiest and strongest at the moment when Death appears beside him to give him his mortal wound. He indeed has reached the greatest point of weakness, with regard both to his bodily strength and to his moral strength. Nevertheless, the inevitable end seems to him particularly unwelcome at this time. As Justice notes in a speech near the end of the play, the representative of the human race who is the hero of the play thought "that he schulde a levyd ay,/ Tyl Deth trypte hym on hys daunce . . ." (ll. 3424-25). The reference is a crucial one, since it makes an essential connection between the manner in which Death comes to Humanum Genus and the way in which he comes to all estates of men and women in the well-known iconography of the Dance of Death.

The tableau that the playwright had in mind at the moment of Humanum Genus' confrontation with Death now may be recognized precisely as a duplication of a scene from the Dance of Death, which shortly was to be most frequently associated with the scenes and verses painted in the cloisters of St. Paul's Cathedral in London (i.e., "the dance of death pictured in Poules" to which More referred) in imitation of the Cemetery of the Holy Innocents in Paris, painted in 1424. The cloisters of St. Paul's had been rebuilt in 1407-21,[15] and at least by the mid-1430's the paintings, complete with verses translated from the French by John Lydgate, monk of Bury St. Edmunds in East Anglia, seem to have been in place.[16] There is no reason to believe that the Dance of Death was not already very well known in England prior to the imitation of the paintings of the Cemetery of the Holy Innocents in the cloisters of St. Paul's,[17] and hence we are not dealing here with the discovery of a particular source for an episode in *The Castle of Perseverance*--a source which indeed would dictate a later date for the play than the other evidence might allow. It is thus far more important to recognize that in *The Castle of Perseverance* the iconography of the Dance of Death enters as a crucial element designed to teach the lesson of man's end--a lesson that was expected to have direct influence on the way in which men and women understand their moral and spiritual condition. In this morality play as also later in *Everyman* for which this iconography likewise plays an important role, the audience is thus expected to learn precisely that which is taught in Lydgate's verses at the beginning of his versification of the Dance of Death:

> O creatures [ye] that ben resonable
> The liff desiryng / which is eternall
> Ye may seen heer / doctrine ful notable
> Your liff to leede / which that is mortall
> Therby to lerne / in especiall
> How ye shal trace / the daunce which that ye see
> To man and wooman / [yliche] naturall
> For deth ne sparith / hih nor lowe degre.[18]

For Lydgate, the Dance of Death is a "myrrour" that reflects the "daunce" that all will dance. There is an element of didacticism here too, though within the context of such a drama as *The Castle of Perseverance* the lesson is more complicated than can be expressed in any merely abstract admonition. The lesson must be given liveliness through the adoption of living dramatic form, which in the case of the figure of Death involves a striking paradox: *Death must seem to come to life as a warning to men and women.* The effectiveness of the allegory, then, depends on its expression of more than an abstract concept; instead, as indicated in the Introduction to this study, the audience must be made to participate vicariously in the action of the play and to respond to the characters as more alive than mere intellectualized ideas.

The figure of Death in the visual arts and in dramas such as *The Castle of Perseverance* invites comparison with an example in the mystery plays, for the Death of Herod in the East Anglian N-town cycle[19] also shows the then familiar representation of Death coming to claim one whose thought has hardly been on his own ending. The theatrical character here is, of course, Herod, who, if we are to believe his lines before Mors enters, is very merry prior to the arrival on the scene of the messenger of God who has come with striking immediacy to punish the proud king for his terrible acts of child murder. "Ow se how prowdely yon kaytyff sytt at mete/ of deth hath he no dowte he wenyth to leve evyr-more," Mors comments (ll. 194-95). With his spear he will kill him "and so cast down his pride" (l. 206). As faithless Herod brags and rejoices over the presumed death of his young rival, the Christ Child, and as his soldiers express their pleasure at their sadistic exploits in the murder of the Holy Innocents, the music of the feast is ordered to strike up. At just this moment Mors kills Herod and his attendant soldiers, whose souls are received by the devil who promises them that now they shall see the "sportys of oure gle"; "of oure myrthis now xal ye se/ and evyr synge welawey" (ll. 243-45). The final description of Mors by himself would appear to correspond perfectly with the illustration of the figure of Death in the visual arts,[20] but it also provides a precise key to understanding the nature of the image:

> Thow I be nakyd and pore of array
> and wurmys knawe me al a-bowte
> Yit loke ye drede me nyth and day
> Ffor whan deth comyth ye stande in dowte
> Evyn lyke to me as I yow say

> shull all ye be here in this rowte
> Whan I yow chalange at my day
> I xal yow make ryght lowe to lowth
>   and nakyd for to be
> Amonges wormys as I yow telle
> Vndyr the erth xul ye dwelle
> and thei xul Etyn both flesch and felle
>   As thei haue don me.
>   (ll. 272-84)

"As I am now, so shall you be," Death in effect is saying, though in moralities such as *The Castle of Perseverance* the emphasis will be on the fate of the soul rather than the body--a fate even more frightening for the individual to contemplate than the hideous decomposition of the body.

The scene with Humanum Genus and Death in *The Castle of Perseverance*, like Everyman and Death in *Everyman* later, performs a specific theatrical function, and it does so by calling up familiar iconography. To be sure, we might have expected the Dance of Death to differentiate between the various classes and conditions of the social order, starting with the most prominent and concluding with the most humble, but this kind of progression is not necessarily present in the tradition. The movement from high to low is, as is well known, present in Lydgate's verses (and, consequently, in the paintings in the cloister of St. Paul's) and in that most famous Dance of Death series, Holbein's *Les simulachres et historiees faces de la mort* (1538). Nevertheless, when the Dance is set forth in a series of this kind, each person receives a separate scene in which he or she is arrested by the figure of Death. Such is the case in the now-lost misericords in St. Michael's Cathedral, Coventry, bombed during World War II, where Death individually arrested a layman of high degree, a pope, a bishop, and others, whom he led away to their end.[21] The actual moment of the arrest is pictured in painted glass in St. Andrew's, Norwich, where a bishop, arrayed in all his vestments and holding a crozier, is isolated as the dread figure of Death appears by his side (fig. 22).[22] The bishop seems no more prepared for his end than Humanum Genus or Everyman, for he turns his head sharply away from the unwelcome intruder in his life. The title pages of

John Skot's editions of *Everyman* (see fig. 23) also provide an example of Death appearing to the individual, since here, as presumably in the play, the grim reaper appears to come to the fashionably dressed representative of all mankind, who raises his hands, resisting the inevitable.[23] In *The Castle of Perseverance* as in *Everyman*, therefore, the Dance is stripped down to the essential action, the arrest of a single individual, Humanum Genus or Everyman, who represents all the orders of society within the play; that individual thus represents all human beings who must face the ultimate confrontation--the termination of life itself.

The collapsing of all the orders of society into one allegorical person, Humanum Genus or Everyman, ought not to seem illogical or artificial. The lesson of the Dance of Death is that all members of all levels of the social order are but one dish at the table of the dissolution of the body. As sermons explained, the "stynkyng dust" of the grave will swallow up all men and women equally. St. Ambrose is said to have insisted: "I dar wel seie the schalt nat perseyve ther any defference betwyx a begger and a kyng, nor betwyx a maister and his knave."[24] Visually, the *transi* tomb, with on one level the unbeautiful figure of the decaying nude body, and on the other the fully dressed body as if living, illustrates the same point. As Gail McMurray Gibson explains with regard to an East Anglian example of such a tomb dated c.1467 at Long Melford, Suffolk, "John Baret's tomb still shocks a casual visitor to St. Mary's church. On the base of the tomb monument, sculpted in low relief, is a portrait of John Baret dressed in a fashionable fifteenth-century robe and a Lancastrian collar. But above reclines a life-size sculpture of death's grim handiwork, a marble corpse, horrible in its decay."[25] An even more impressive example, though not from East Anglia, is the tomb of Henry Chichele in Canterbury Cathedral.[26] Above in the normal position for the sepulchral effigy is the fully clothed and idealized figure of the archbishop (d. 1443) with hands in prayer. His mitred head rests on a pillow, beside which the carver placed small figures of angels. Such was the man in his earthly achievement, highly placed in the hierarchy of the Church and the spiritual leader of England. But all men, including the Archbishop of Canterbury, must come to the same end--an end which is graphically displayed on the lower level of the tomb. Here is another figure of Archbishop Chichele with features recognizably like those on the top of the tomb. But the archbishop in this instance, nude and lying on his grave clothes, appears in all the ugliness of death, with his body distorted and grotesque in its decay. The lesson is that all human hands smell of mortality--and they smell equally. Also, more importantly, before the bar of justice at the Last Judgment, archbishops and kings will have no priority, but all will be treated on a fair and equal basis by the judge.[27] Illustrations which show the Last Judgment often set forth the humble and the great grouped on both the left and right sides of Christ--i.e., among both the damned and those receiving salvation.

The importance of the beginning and the end of all time for our understanding of death's role in life cannot be overestimated. Holbein's *Dance of Death* series opens with a woodcut showing God the Creator in the Garden at the creation of Eve (sig. B4v)--a scene that is quickly followed by the Fall (sig. C1r) and Expulsion from the Garden (sig. C1v). Here is the gate by which Death came into the world, entering through man's original disobedience, an act which has established for all time the lapsarian condition to which the race is heir. As Death in *Everyman* explains, "in the worlde eche lyuynge creature/ For Adams synne must dye of nature" (ll. 144-45). Because of this fact, God has seen the need to rescue mankind through the Incarnation and Crucifixion, both events that intersect historical time. Thus the groundwork has been laid for a final divine intersection in history--the Last Judgment--when those who have transcended death's sting will be, like Adam himself at the Harrowing, released from the powers of darkness into light. In any case, the Holbein series appropriately ends with a woodcut showing the Day of Doom (sig. G4r), followed by an armorial of Death that includes a coat of arms with a skull and a crest with an hourglass atop a helmet as well as skeletal arms holding a stone (sig. G4v). This *memento mori*, observed in the woodcut by a gentleman on the left and a lady on the right, serves as a reminder to all men and women that life should be lived in the temporal presence of death at every moment. As the poet of *Everyman* explains, "after dethe, amendes may no man make,/ For than mercy and pyte doth hym forsake" (ll. 912-13). The danger of being among those who will be tossed into the everlasting bonfire is very real; only grace, as extended through the Church, was believed to serve as a way of rescue from such an eternal end. And, as *Mankind* especially sets out to demonstrate, the principle through which the Church functions to extend such heavenly grace is *mercy*, "the very mene for [mankind's] restytucyon" (l. 17).

The phenomenological consequence of contemplating the historical beginning and the end, therefore, depends upon the contemporary insistence on the significance of the redemptive process set forward at the center of history. This process, as we have noted, also was believed to involve a death--the death at the Crucifixion of one in place of many ("Yt may be seyde and veryfyede, mankynde was dere bought./ By the pytuose deth of Jhesu he hade hys remedye," Mercy explains in *Mankind*, ll. 9-10). The problem would seem to have been to force recognition of this point upon an audience or congregation. In *Everyman*, God complains:

> My lawe that I shewed, whan I for them dyed,
> They forgete clene / and shedyng of my blode rede.
> I hanged bytwene two theues, it can not be denyed;
> To gete them lyfe I suffred to be deed;
> I heled theyr fete / with thornes hurt was my heed.
> I coude do no more than I dyde, truely;
> And nowe I se the people do clene for-sake me.
>   (ll. 29-35)

In the early sixteenth-century morality *Hick Scorner*, one of the characters also remarks:

> think what God did for thee!
> On Good Friday he hanged on a tree,
> And all his precious blood spent.
> A spear did rive his heart asunder.
> The gates he brake up with a clap of thunder,
> And Adam and Eve there delivered he.
>   (ll. 942-47)[28]

This passage, we should note, is of considerable significance, since it reveals an aspect of popular theology that is surely more important than has previously been recognized with regard to the structure and iconography of the morality plays. Together the historical Crucifixion and the legendary Harrowing of Hell provide the means through which release from the otherwise unbreakable cycle of death is seen to be made possible. These displays of God's mercy are important because without them the confrontation with death could lead only to the unalleviated terror of despair. In *The Castle of Perseverance*, therefore, the resolution of the argument among the Four Daughters of God must provide the basis for a happy conclusion in the drama. In *Everyman*, on the other hand, the function of grace in this world through the sacramental system of the Church is to alleviate despair and to secure safe passage for the soul at the end of life's journey. In *Mankind* and in other pre-Reformation morality plays, mercy serves as the key to achieving a satisfactory life, which, we are assured, will nevertheless involve a confrontation in the end with the reality of death. Such a confrontation is the case in the earliest English morality, *The Pride of Life*, which was most likely written early in the third quarter of the fourteenth century.[29]

The Pride of Life is only a fragment, but we know its plot through the summary presented in the speech of the Prolocutor at the beginning of the play. The King of Life, assisted by his counselors Strength and Health, is a strongly masculine champion of pride which defies all fear, including that of death. "I schal lyue evermo/ And croun þer as kinge," he brags; "I ne may neuer wit of wo,/ I lyue at my likinge" (ll. 175-79). His queen urges a more cautious and respectful attitude toward life, toward God, and toward the Church, but, calling her by an Anglo-Norman term of endearment--"Douce dam"--he nevertheless continues to insist on his immortality while additionally insinuating that she may merely wish him dead. The idea that "Deth ouercomith al thinge" (l. 205) is, he says, only a feminine "tale" (l. 209). Such bragging must also have a comic side, since the king's claims are so patently absurd. The king's predicament is indeed reminiscent of Lucifer's bragging in the opening plays of the English Creation to Doom play cycles, for like Lucifer the speaker's words defy reality in their insistence upon his immortality and omnipotence.

LIFE'S TERMINUS

The King of Life must sleep, however, and at this time his queen takes the initiative in sending for the bishop who will lecture him on the dangers of his current attitude and way of life. This clergyman calls upon his royal audience to recognize his own humanity; as a man, he came naked into the world, and so also will he someday reach the end of his life--a time when his five wits will at last desert him. Furthermore, if overtaken by death in all the arrogance of youth (for the king in his pride is clearly young), he will find a worse consequence--death separated from the light of heaven. The bishop threatens:

> Thot thou leu now as the list,
>   Det wol cum rit son,
> And giue the dethis wounde
>   For thin outrage;
> Within a litil stounde
>   Then artou but a page.
> Qwhen thou art grauen on grene,
>   Ther metis fleys and molde,
> Then helpith litil, I wene,
>   Thi gay croun of golde. (ll. 437-46)

Ironically, the king's response is to send for Death in order to challenge him to combat. This combat is, unfortunately, not recorded in the text because the fragment breaks off.

The speech of the Prolocutor, however, explains what now will happen. As we expect, the king will fight with the allegorical figure of Death, and he will lose. Death must spare no one. The King of Life, because of his arrogance and pride, must now find his soul taken away to the realm of the fiends. Nevertheless, in spite of his loss to the victor Death, the story of the king is not yet ended. Mercy will still have its day. Our Lady, the Blessed Virgin Mary, whose role in the Judgment frequently appears in the visual arts,[30] prays successfully to her Son for mercy for the king's soul.

The allegorical shape of Death which appears in *The Pride of Life*, *The Castle of Perseverance*, and, later, *Everyman* is, as we have seen, a familiar iconographic type. From about the middle of the thirteenth century, this emblem of death had become fairly well fixed as a visible sign of the cessation of life, and in its precise visual form tended to reflect the growing popularity of embalming.[31] As noted above, interest in death would indeed rise sharply during the period following the great plague years of 1348-49, though we now know that some of the pessimistic attitudes that are associated with these years had already become rooted as early as the beginning of the fourteenth century.[32] The Dance of Death not surprisingly is to be identified as a particular theme that caught people's imaginations in the aftermath of the terrible onslaught of the plague years when the population of Britain was substantially reduced by pestilence. Likewise, it would appear that *The Pride of Life*, which came down to us on a portion of some accounts from the Priory of the Holy Trinity, Dublin, for the dates 30 June 1343 to 5 January 1344, was a product of the period that came immediately after the introduction of the pestilence of the bubonic plague into the British Isles.[33]

But the understanding of the figure of Death in the early morality drama also suggests the usefulness of examining another iconographic motif, the related subject of the Three Living and the Three Dead,[34] in spite of the fact that this iconography does not appear directly in the plays. Nevertheless, the motif provides an important iconographic context which reflects some significant attitudes that during this time are shared with the morality plays, for here the concerns of life and death are brought into focus as if in a single image. Life implies what is beyond life. In English wall painting (e.g., in the example over the chancel arch of the church at Packwood, Warwickshire), this scene was very popular as a warning against the complacency that was believed to overcome people satisfied with their earthly lives.[35] In its various forms, the subject illustrates three living men, sometimes representing (like the three Magi) three ages of man from youth to age, who come face to face with three corpses. The corpses are reflections of their own fate. In an illumination (fig. 24) to which convenient reference may be made in the De Lisle Psalter, the illuminator has inscribed above the living kings the following: "I am afert"; "Lo whet ich se"; "Methinketh hit beth deueles thre." And above the dead is written: "Ich wes wel fair"; "Such scheltou be"; "For godes loue be wer by me" (fol. 127).[36]

Death, therefore, may be defined as coming from within the

body. The three living see as in a mirror their end, which is depicted very much like the grotesque cadaver included in the *transi* tomb. So also in the figure of Mors that appears to the King of Life, Humanum Genus, Everyman, or the Herod of the N-town play is the dissolution of the body displayed--a bodily dissolution that fortunately may be transcended at the Last Day if one is able to find himself or herself on the right hand rather than at the left hand of God. Death as personified in the plays from *The Pride of Life*, preceding the earliest of the Macro moralities, through the later *Everyman* may on one level be the messenger (or champion) who announces one's death to a man or woman, but on another level he is a very precise reflection of the immediacy of death and of the transitory nature of the human condition itself. Previously in this study reference has been made to the Ash Wednesday liturgy, which reminds men that they were made from dust and to dust shall they return--and this statement is one that was universally regarded as central to any accurate understanding of human existence. As Everyman explains at the side of the grave, "in to this caue must I crepe/ And tourne to erth, and there to slepe" (ll. 792-93). A graffito, found at Gamlingay, provides another perspective: "Death is like a shadow which always follows the body."[37] Yet, fearful as the death of the body and its physical dissolution are, the playwrights, like their contemporaries, felt that an even more terrifying prospect is the soul's ultimate confrontation with the Judge who is Christ, who will determine each person's eternal condition thereafter.

Dying thus takes place always in the presence of the ultimate forces of the universe. A continental woodcut, in the *Ars Moriendi* published at Florence in 1494, usefully illustrates the condition of the dying man:[38] above is God in heaven, with the angels of the Apocalypse blowing their horrid trumpets to the four corners of the earth; below is hell, with the devil clutching small souls in his right and left hands to show his sadistic control over the damned. The dying man, fashionably dressed and surely in a mood not unlike that intended to be represented in the woodcut figure of Everyman on the title pages of Skot's editions of the play,[39] looks down as he stands on the very rim of hell beside a skeletal figure of Death with his scythe. Death's summons precipitates the greatest crisis in the life of man--a crisis which is capable of being profoundly exploited as part of the stage spectacle.

But unlike the Herod in the N-town play, the morality figures who confront Death fare surprisingly well. For example, Everyman, as he sets forth on his journey to the undiscovered country beyond death, receives assurance that "all shall be well" (l. 693). These significant words, spoken by Discretion, echo a resounding faith in transcendence--a faith which has been compared to the trust a child, awakening from a nightmare, finds in a comforting parent.[40] Having repented and put on the garment of contrition, Everyman will now also receive the "holy sacrament and oyntement togyder" (l. 709). He has made out his will, giving half of his goods to charity and the rest "to be retourned there it ought to be" (l. 702). Assisted by repentance, the Eucharist, and extreme unction, he will come at last to his grave, where he will be deserted by Beauty, Strength, Discretion, and Five Wits. There is a moment of terror, which is overcome only by an awareness of transcendence: "O, all thynge fayleth, saue God alone" (l. 841). Indeed, when Everyman actually descends into the grave, only Good Deeds accompanies him. Everyman's final words commend his soul into God's hands in terms that imitate the words of Christ on the cross. The death of the penitent man thus repeats in some sense the death of the Savior. Quite clearly Everyman is now ready to render up his accounts at the final scene of reckoning.[41] That the ultimate audit will be satisfactory is shown by the words of the angel who, echoing the antiphon *Veni electa mea*,[42] says:

> Come, excellente electe spouse, to Iesu!
> Here aboue thou shalte go
> Bycause of thy synguler vertue.
> Now thy soule is taken thy body fro,
> Thy rekenynge is crystall-clere.
> Now shalte thou in to the heuenly spere,
> Vnto the whiche all ye shall come
> That lyueth well before the daye of dome.
> (ll. 894-901)

Though Everyman's body is asleep in his grave, his soul is nevertheless safe. The iconography is familiar in the visual arts, where the angel takes up a small doll-like soul in a napkin to save it from the clutches of fiends who sometimes stand by with malicious hope. As an example of this iconography, we may cite a woodcarving of c.1470 on the central roof of the choir of All Saints, North Street, York; here an angel takes up the tonsured figure of a naked soul, possibly that of the donor, John Gylliot.[43] Even more explicit is the illustration placed at the end of "Of the Seven Ages" in British Library MS. Add. 37,049, fol. 29, which shows the fiend standing in expectation while a ministering angel rescues the soul of the dying man who is lying in his bed (fig. 11).

However, *The Castle of Perseverance* dramatizes what is an even more frightening situation, for here the soul of Humanum Genus is actually taken away by the evil angel, who along with his companions will see that he is punished with the severest suffering. Nevertheless, here too mercy will overcome all obstacles, and in the end God, sitting on his throne, will announce a different judgment--"Not aftyr deseruynge to do reddere,/ To dampne Mankynde to turmentry,/ But brynge hym to my blysse ful clere/ In heuene to dwelle endelesly . . ." (ll. 3565-68). Hereupon he will send his Four Daughters, who are now reconciled, to bring Humanum Genus to heaven where he will achieve bliss through the extension of divine mercy. Such mercy overcomes both Sin and Death, and so it shall also be at the Last Judgment when the trumpet shall sound and the dead arise. At the conclusion of the drama, therefore, it seems altogether appropriate that the Father should turn to the audience and announce the ending of "oure gamys" with an admonition to everyone to "Thynke on youre last endynge" (ll. 3645, 3648).

Mankind likewise concludes with the character of Mercy reminding people of God's mercy and the potential reward of bliss which may be achieved on the other side of the barrier of death. The alternative would be for the soul to be burned like chaff in perpetual fire following the binary separation of souls at the Last Day. *Wisdom*, on the other hand, emphasizes in its conclusion the return to wisdom which the experiences of contrition and devotion are able to achieve within the context of mystical Christianity; but renewal in grace is also indeed the prelude to a good ending and can take place only when the person is aware of the ultimate

LIFE'S TERMINUS

realities of life--i.e., of Death and its consequences. Instead of taking part in "the Deullys dance" (l. 700) which will lead directly to the mouth of hell following the blowing of the trumpets at the Last Judgment (see l. 702),[44] the soul and its faculties need instead to look for help toward the wisdom that will assist in the rejection of those bodily motions and those thoughts which would in the end prove destructive. The Macro plays without exception, therefore, teach the ultimate wisdom summed up by the figure of the Carthusian who, in words supplied by the monk Lydgate of Bury St. Edmunds in his *Dance of Death*, responds to the Death with resignation and a full knowledge of man's condition:

Vn-to this world/ I was de[d] ago ful longe
Bi myn ordre / and my profession
[Thowgh] euery man / be he neuyr so strong
Dredith to deye / bi naturall mocion
Afftyr his Flesshly / inclynacion
Plese it [the] lorde / my sowle for to borwe
Fro feendis myht / and from dampnacion
Som arn to-day / that shal nat be to-morwe.[45]

NOTES

INTRODUCTION

1. See Margaret Rickert, *Painting in Britain: The Middle Ages*, 2nd ed. (Harmondsworth: Penguin, 1965), pp. 123-35.
2. *Records of Plays and Players in Norfolk and Suffolk*, ed. David Galloway and John Wasson, Malone Soc. Collections, IX (1980-81); *Norwich, 1540-1652*, ed. David Galloway, Records of Early English Drama (Toronto: Univ. of Toronto Press, 1984); Ian Lancashire, *Dramatic Texts and Records of Britain: A Chronological Topography to 1558* (Toronto: Univ. of Toronto Press, 1984), *passim*. Further research in the dramatic records of this region is in progress under the auspices of Records of Early English Drama at the University of Toronto.
3. *The Late Medieval Religious Plays of Bodleian MSS Digby 133 and e museo 160*, ed. Donald C. Baker, John L. Murphy, and Louis B. Hall, EETS, 283 (1982), pp. xiii-xiv, xix, xxxvi; *Ludus Coventriae, or The Plai called Corpus Christi* [N-Town Cycle], ed. K. S. Block, EETS, e.s. 120 (1922); see also especially Gail McMurray Gibson, "Bury St. Edmunds, Lydgate, and the N-Town Cycle," *Speculum*, 56 (1981), 56-90, and Richard Beadle, "The Medieval Drama of East Anglia: Studies in Dialect, Documentary Records and Stagecraft," Ph.D. thesis (Univ. of York, 1977), *passim*.
4. William Prideaux Courtney, "Cox Macro," *DNB*, XII, 727-28. Macro's volume containing the plays was inherited by John Patteson of Norwich, who in 1819 sold it and other manuscripts from the collection to a local bookseller, Richard Beatniffe. Beatniffe then sold the manuscripts the next year through Christie's.
5. Stephen Spector, "Paper Evidence and the Genesis of the Macro Plays," *Mediaevalia*, 5 (1979), 217-32, and David Bevington, ed., *The Macro Plays* (New York: Johnson Reprint; Folger Shakespeare Library, 1972), p. xvii.
6. *DNB*, XII, 728; Bevington, ed., *Macro Plays*, p. xvii. Gurney purchased the manuscript containing the Macro plays in the sale at Christie's. The plays were removed from their nineteenth-century binding in 1971 when the pages were photographed for Bevington's facsimile

NOTES

edition.

7. The signature appears on fols. 121 and 134; see W. K. Smart, *Some English and Latin Sources and Parallels for the Morality of Wisdom* (Menasha, Wisconsin: George Banta, 1912), p. 86; Mark Eccles, ed., *The Macro Plays*, EETS, 262 (1969), pp. xxvii-xxviii; Gail McMurray Gibson, "The Play of *Wisdom* and the Abbey of St. Edmund," *Comparative Drama*, 19 (1985), 118 (rpt. in *The* Wisdom *Symposium*, ed. Milla Cozart Riggio [New York: AMS Press, 1986], pp. 40-41). Thomas Hyngham, monachus, of Bury St. Edmunds similarly signed an untraced Boethius; see N. R. Ker, *Medieval Libraries of Great Britain: A List of Surviving Books*, 2nd ed. (London: Royal Historical Soc., 1964), p. 234. For the glass at Long Melford, see Christopher Woodforde, *The Norwich School of Glass-Painting in the Fifteenth Century* (London: Oxford Univ. Press, 1950), p. 112, and especially Gibson, "Bury St. Edmunds, Lydgate, and the N-Town cycle," p. 80. In 1688, an inscription in the painted glass requested prayers for "Hengham, nuper Abbatis de Bury," and although the inscription is lost, the figure of the abbot remains, kneeling before the image of St. Edmund in the glass. Such a portrait of a fifteenth-century owner of play manuscripts is surely unique, if indeed the "Hyngham" of the Macro manuscript is the same man as Thomas Hyngham, Abbot of Bury St. Edmunds. For the suggestion that Hyngham may merely have been a scribe, see Richard Beadle, "The Scribal Problem in the Macro Manuscript," *English Language Notes*, 21, No. 4 (1984), 12.

8. For a list of books known to be from the monastery, see Ker, *Medieval Libraries*, pp. 16-22.

9. Bevington, ed., *Macro Plays*, p. xvii.

10. See Donald C. Baker, "The Date of Mankind," *Philological Quarterly*, 42 (1963), 90-91, and Eccles, ed., *Macro Plays*, p. xxxviii; on the date of the manuscript, cf. Spector, "Paper Evidence," p. 219. For *The Castle of Perseverance*, the date of the copy has been usually placed at c.1440, though the play is undoubtedly older, perhaps dating from the first quarter of the fifteenth century. See A. W. Pollard's Introduction to Frederick Furnivall's edition of *The Macro Plays*, EETS, e.s. 91 (1904), pp. xxxi-xxxii; Spector, "Paper Evidence," p. 224; Eccles, ed., *Macro Plays*, pp. x-xi; Bevington, ed., *Macro Plays*, p. viii. Only Jacob Bennett dates the play prior to 1400; see his article "The 'Castle of Perserverance': Redactions, Place, and Date," *Mediaeval Studies*, 24 (1962), 141-52.

11. See Eccles, ed., *Macro Plays*, p. xxx; on the date of the manuscript, see Spector, "Paper Evidence," p. 223. But see Gibson, "The Play of *Wisdom* and the Abbey of St. Edmund," pp. 130-31. Gibson (p.

NOTES

132) also cites Beadle's suggestion that Hyngham "or someone who wrote very similarly" may have been the scribe who wrote this segment of the Macro manuscript; see Beadle, "The Scribal Problem," p. 9.

12. Galloway and Wasson, *Records of Plays and Players in Norfolk and Suffolk*, esp. pp. 147-48 for the Bury region, and see also the more general comments in John Wasson, "The Morality Play: Ancestor of Elizabethan Drama?" *Comparative Drama*, 13 (1979), 210-21 (rpt. in *Drama in the Middle Ages*, ed. Clifford Davidson, C. J. Gianakaris, and John H. Stroupe [New York: AMS Press, 1982], pp. 316-27).

13. See Pamela Sheingorn, "The Visual Language of Drama," in *Contexts of Early English Drama*, ed. Marianne Briscoe and John Coldewey (Bloomington: Indiana Univ. Press, forthcoming), for the observation that medieval drama when staged is to be regarded as one of the visual arts. See additionally the comments on methodology in my handbook: *Drama and Art: An Introduction to the Use of Evidence from the Visual Arts for the Study of Early Drama*, Early Drama, Art, and Music, Monograph Ser., 1 (Kalamazoo: Medieval Institute, 1977).

14. Richard Southern, *The Medieval Theatre in the Round*, 2nd ed. (New York: Theatre Arts, 1975), *passim*.

15. Wasson, "The Morality Play: Ancestor of Elizabethan Drama?" pp. 210-21.

16. See Robert Potter, *The English Morality Play* (London: Routledge and Kegan Paul, 1975), pp. 193-212.

17. William Hone, *Ancient Mysteries Described* (London, 1823), p. 227.

18. Ibid., p. x.

19. Thomas Sharp, *A Dissertation on the Pageants or Dramatic Mysteries anciently performed at Coventry* (Coventry, 1825; rpt. East Ardsley, Wakefield: EP Publishing, 1973), pp. 22-23.

20. Ibid., p. 23.

21. John Payne Collier, *History of English Dramatic Poetry to the Time of Shakespeare* (1831; rpt. New York: AMS Press, 1970), II, 279-97.

22. Ibid., II, 287n. *Wisdom* is the only one of the Macro plays to appear in a text in another manuscript; see *The Late Medieval Religious Plays of Bodleian MSS Digby 133 and e museo 160*, ed. Baker et al., pp. 116-40. See also the comments of Donald C. Baker and John L. Murphy on the fragment of *Wisdom* in the Digby manuscript in "The Late Medieval Plays of MS Digby 133: Scribes, Dates, and Early History," *Research Opportunities in Renaissance Drama*, 10 (1967), 156, 161, 163-64. The connection of Digby MS. 133 with the Bury St. Edmunds

NOTES

area and the possibility that the fragment of *Wisdom* also came from the monastery would seem to strengthen the case for regarding the Macro manuscript as most likely from the monastery as well.

23. See Potter, *English Morality Play*, pp. 213-14.
24. Collier, *History of English Dramatic Poetry*, II, 259.
25. Ibid., II, 259.
26. Ibid., II, 260.
27. Ibid., II, 260.
28. Thomas Warton, *History of English Poetry* (1778), II, 365, as quoted by Potter, *English Morality Play*, p. 208. For a well informed interpretation, see especially Alan J. Fletcher, "The Meaning of 'gostly to owr purpos' in *Mankind*," *Notes and Queries*, 31 (1984), 301-02.
29. Cf., however, Arnold Williams, "The English Moral Play before 1500," *Annuale Mediaevale*, 4 (1963), 18.
30. Cf. ibid., p. 22. See also E. N. S. Thompson, "The English Moral Plays," *Transactions of the Connecticut Academy of Arts and Sciences*, 16 (1910), pp. 293-312. For a recent study which usefully treats the technique of the moralities as they provide an internalized framework for memory or "spiritual 'seeing'," see Stanton Garner, Jr., "Theatricality in *Mankind* and *Everyman*," *Studies in Philology*, 84 (1987), 276.
31. *Comparative Drama*, 12 (1978), 23-34 (rpt. in *Drama in the Middle Ages*, ed. Davidson, Gianakaris, and Stroupe, pp. 304-15).
32. *English Morality Play*, esp. p. 34: "The characters of the morality plays, though fitted out with abstract names, are impersonated by human actors. This obvious fact (generally the major discovery in any modern production) adds a dimension of humanity to the most theological of moralities. At the center stands a figure (or figures) representing humanity; to him, in turn, come auxiliary figures--persuasive agents of temptation and earnest agents of repentance. The pattern is such that both, in their ways, will be convincing."

See also the comments of Joanne Spencer Kantrowitz, *Dramatic Allegory: Lindsay's Ane Satyre of the Thrie Estaitis* (Lincoln: Univ. of Nebraska Press, 1975), pp. 131-45.

33. William Flint Thrall and Addison Hibbard, *A Handbook to Literature* (New York: Odyssey Press, 1960), pp. 7-8.
34. Paul Piehler, *The Visionary Landscape* (London: Edward Arnold, 1971), p. 11.
35. Samuel Taylor Coleridge, *The Complete Works*, ed. W. G. T. Shedd (New York: Harper, 1884), I, 437-38.
36. Ibid., pp. 437-38.

NOTES

37. John Wyclif, *The English Works*, ed. F. D. Matthew, EETS, o.s. 74 (1880), pp. 429-30; the passage is believed to be an interpolation by the translator. See also Alexandra F. Johnston, "The Plays of the Religious Guilds of York: The Creed Play and the Pater Noster Play," *Speculum*, 50 (1975), 70-80.

38. See Schmitt, "Idea of a Person," p. 30.

39. See Potter, *English Morality Play*, p. 34.

40. Erwin Panofsky, *Early Netherlandish Painting* (1953; rpt. New York: Harper and Row, 1971), I, 141.

41. *Summa Theologiae*, I, Question I, Art. 9c, as quoted by Panofsky, *Early Netherlandish Painting*, I, 142.

42. *Areopagitica*; see Ray Heffner, Dorothy E. Mason, Frederick M. Padelford, *Spenser Allusions in the Sixteenth and Seventeenth Centuries*, ed. William Wells, Studies in Philology, 69, No. 5 (1972), p. 215.

43. Records of additional extant, lost, and fragmentary examples of the morality play in the fifteenth century are listed in Lancashire, *Dramatic Texts and Records*; these include the Lincoln Pater Noster play, the Beverley Pater Noster play, "A Dramatic Monologue by Law" (*Secular Lyrics of the XIVth and XVth Centuries*, ed. R. H. Robbins [Oxford, 1955], pp. 110-14), Thomas Chaundler's *Liber Apologeticus* (ed. Doris Enright-Clark Shoukri [London, 1974]), the Winchester Interludes (*Occupation and Idleness*, and *Lucidus and Dubius*; see the facsimile and transcription in *Non-Cycle Plays and the Winchester Dialogues*, ed. Norman Davis, Leeds Texts and Monographs, Medieval Drama Facsimiles, 5 [Leeds: Univ. of Leeds, School of English, 1979], pp. 133-208), "lusorum vocato le capp mayntenaunce" from Magdalen College, Oxford (R. E. Alton, "The Academic Drama in Oxford: Extracts from the Records of Four Colleges," *Malone Society Collections*, V [1960], 44), and "ludo de Mankynd" from East Retford, Notts. (Wenzel, "An Early Reference to a Corpus Christi Play," *Modern Philology*, 74 [1977], 390-94).

44. Introduction, *Macro Plays*, ed. Furnivall, p. xviii.

45. W. Roy Mackenzie, *The English Moralities from the Point of View of Allegory* (1914; rpt. New York: Gordian Press, 1966), p. 65.

46. Hardin Craig, *English Religious Drama of the Middle Ages* (Oxford: Clarendon Press, 1955), p. 350.

47. David Bevington, *From Mankind to Marlowe* (Cambridge: Harvard Univ. Press, 1962), p. 18.

48. Eccles, ed., *Macro Plays*, p. xlv.

49. Lawrence M. Clopper, "Mankind and Its Audience," *Comparative Drama*, 8 (1974-75), 347-55.

NOTES

50. Ibid., p. 354.

51. Paula Neuss, "Active and Idle Language: Dramatic Images *Mankind*," in *Medieval Drama*, ed. Neville Denny, Stratford-upon-Avon Studies, 16 (London: Edward Arnold, 1973), pp. 41-67; Kathleen Ashley, "Titivillus and the Battle of Words in *Mankind*," *Annuale Mediaevale*, 16 (1975), 128-50.

52. Neuss, "Active and Idle Language," p. 42; on visual elements in the Macro plays, see also Michael R. Kelley, *Flamboyant Drama* (Carbondale and Edwardsville: Southern Illinois Univ. Press, 1979). Kelley is interested in stylistic rather than iconographic features of these plays.

53. See also Siegfried Wenzel, *The Sin of Sloth:* Acedia (Chapel Hill: Univ. of North Carolina Press, 1967), pp. 150-55.

54. See Chapter I, below.

55. A. W. Pollard had included a selection of only 408 lines of *The Castle of Perseverance* in his anthology, *English Miracle Plays, Moralities, and Interludes* (Oxford: Clarendon Press, 1890).

56. *Macro Plays*, ed. Furnivall, p. xxvi.

57. Mackenzie, *English Moralities*, p. 58. For a less enthusiastic recent view of the play, see W. A. Davenport, *Fifteenth-Century English Drama* (Cambridge: D. S. Brewer, 1982), pp. 106ff.

58. Thompson, "English Moral Plays," pp. 312, 320.

59. See E. K. Chambers, *The Mediaeval Stage* (London: Oxford Univ. Press, 1903), I, 154-55, and Thompson, "English Moral Plays," pp. 320-33.

60. See Wolfgang Riehle, *The Middle English Mystics*, trans. Bernard Standring (London: Routledge and Kegan Paul, 1981), pp. 13-23.

61. Introduction, *Macro Plays*, ed. Furnivall, p. xxii.

62. Arnold Williams, *The Drama of Medieval England* (East Lansing: Michigan State Univ. Press, 1961), p. 148.

63. Eccles, ed., *Macro Plays*, p. xxxvi.

64. Ibid., p. xxxvi.

65. Eugene D. Hill, "The Trinitarian Allegory of the Moral Play of *Wisdom*," *Modern Philology*, 73 (1975), 121-35. For a review of critical opinion of this play, see Sheila Lindenbaum, "The Morality Plays," in *A Manual of the Writings in Middle English*, ed. Albert E. Hartung (New Haven: Connecticut Academy of Arts and Sciences, 1975), V, 1369-71.

66. David Bevington, "'Blake and wyght, fowll and fayer': Stage Picture in *Wisdom Who Is Christ*," *Comparative Drama*, 19 (1985), 136-50 (rpt. in *The* Wisdom *Symposium*, ed. Riggio, pp. 18-38); Milla

NOTES

Riggio, "The Staging of *Wisdom*," *Research Opportunities in Renaissance Drama*, 17 (1984), 167-76 (rpt. in *The* Wisdom *Symposium*, pp. 1-17); and Theresa Coletti and Pamela Sheingorn, "Playing *Wisdom* at Trinity College," in the same issue of *Research Opportunities in Renaissance Drama*, pp. 179-84.

67. Potter, *English Morality Play*, pp. 8ff. Such a view of the moralities is surely more sound than the conventional one which would stress the role of these dramas in emancipating drama from religion and preparing the way for Elizabethan drama; the latter view has not been eradicated (see Sumiko Miyajima, *The Theatre of Man: Dramatic Technique and Stagecraft in the English Medieval Moral Plays* [Clevedon: Clevedon Printing, 1977], pp. 1-5).

68. See Willard Farnham, *The Medieval Heritage of Elizabethan Tragedy* (1936; rpt. Oxford: Basil Blackwell, 1963), pp. 202-05; Carl J. Stratman, "*Everyman*: The Way to Death; or, Eternal Salvation," *Drama Critique*, 7 (1964), 61-64; and Allen D. Goldhamer, "*Everyman*: A Dramatization of Death," *Classica et Mediaevalia*, 30 (1969), 595-616.

69. Gillian Cohen, *The Psychology of Cognition* (London: Academic Press, 1977), pp. 26-45.

70. F. P. Pickering, *Literature and Art in the Middle Ages* (Coral Gables, Florida: Univ. of Miami Press, 1970), *passim*.

71. See the cautions expressed by A. M. Nagler, *The Medieval English Stage* (New Haven: Yale Univ. Press, 1976), p. xi. Nagler's position is, to be sure, quite different from mine with regard to the usefulness of the visual arts and iconography (cf. ibid., pp. 74-105). Nevertheless, it would seem to be wise in this study to avoid the kind of reconstruction which has for very good reason made Southern's *Medieval Theatre in the Round* so very controversial.

For a recent attempt to establish parallels between a morality play's scenes and wall painting, see John Edwards, "The Mural and the Morality Play: A Suggested Source for the Wall-Painting at Oddington," *Transactions of the Bristol and Gloucestershire Archaeological Society*, 104 (1986), 187-200.

NOTES

CHAPTER I:
MANKIND: SOWING AND REAPING

1. Cf. Richard Southern, *The Staging of Plays Before Shakespeare* (London: Faber and Faber, 1973), pp. 21-45. Southern's methodology, which ignores iconographic traditions, is thus somewhat lacking in sophistication, though his suggestions are frequently useful to directors and producers and should be taken into account by anyone planning to mount a production of *Mankind*.

2. See Morris P. Tilley, *A Dictionary of Proverbs in England in the Sixteenth and Seventeenth Centuries* (Ann Arbor: Univ. of Michigan Press, 1950), No. S 687; cf. *Galatians* 6.7.

3. *The Sarum Missal*, ed. J. Wickham Legg (Oxford: Clarendon Press, 1916), p. 47.

4. *Speculum Sacerdotale*, ed. Edward H. Weatherly, EETS, o.s. 200 (1936), p. 50.

5. Ibid., pp. 51-52.

6. Madeline Harrison Caviness, *The Windows of Christ Church Cathedral, Canterbury*, Corpus Vitrearum Medii Aevi, Great Britain, 2 (London: Oxford Univ. Press, 1981), pp. 120-22, fig. 199, and *The Early Stained Glass of Canterbury Cathedral* (Princeton: Princeton Univ. Press, 1977), pp. 63-65, fig. 89.

7. Compare the illumination in Herrad of Landsberg, *Hortus Deliciarum*, ed. Aristide D. Caratzas (New Rochelle, N.Y.: Caratzas, 1977), fol. 108^v.

8. Cf. Sister Mary Philippa Coogan, *An Interpretation of the Moral Play*, Mankind (Washington: Catholic Univ. of America Press, 1947), *passim*.

9. Noted by Coogan, p. 8. See also *Sarum Breviary* (1531), Calendar (STC 15830). Quotations from the Macro plays in my text are from the edition of Eccles except where otherwise noted. I have, however, regularized the thorn and yogh as these appear in Eccles' edition to conform with modern practice for typographical reasons.

10. G. L. Remnant, *A Catalogue of Misericords in Great Britain* (Oxford: Clarendon Press, 1969), p. 168. See also, however, the wall painting at Longthorpe Tower near Peterborough, described by E. W. Tristram, *English Wall Painting of the Fourteenth Century* (London: Routledge and Kegan Paul, 1955), p. 220; here, as not uncommonly is the case in English iconography, March is represented by a man digging. In

138

NOTES

contrast to continental representations, the English artists very frequently chose sowing and digging as emblems for this month; see James Fowler, "On Mediaeval Representations of the Months and Seasons," *Archaeologia*, 44 (1873), 137-77, and James Carson Webster, *The Labors of the Months in Antique and Medieval Art* (1938; rpt. New York: AMS Press, 1970), pp. 88-93.

11. See *The Oxford Dictionary of the Christian Church*, ed. F. L. Cross, 2nd ed. (Oxford: Oxford Univ. Press, 1974), p. 1193.

12. Coogan, *An Interpretation*, pp. 5-6.

13. See ibid., pp. 1-21.

14. Douglas Gray, "The Five Wounds of Our Lord--III," *Notes and Queries*, 208 (1963), 127-34.

15. Émile Mâle, *Religious Art in France: The Late Middle Ages*, trans. Marthiel Matthews and ed. Harry Bober, Bollingen Ser., 90, Pt. 3 (Princeton: Princeton Univ. Press, 1986), figs. 60-63. See also Evelyn Underhill, "The Fountain of Life: An Iconological Study," *Burlington Magazine*, 19 (1910), 99-109, and James H. Marrow, *Passion Iconography in Northern European Art of the Late Middle Ages and Early Renaissance* (Kortrijk: Van Ghemmert, 1979), p. 139, Pl. facing p. 58.

16. Gray, "Five Wounds," p. 127.

17. *Speculum Sacerdotale*, pp. 51-52.

18. Ibid., p. 52. Sometimes the seventh Act is not illustrated; such is the case in the well-known painted glass at All Saints, North Street, York (see F. Harrison, *The Painted Glass of York* [London: SPCK, 1927], Pl. facing p. 180). See also the illustration of the Corporal Acts in the Judgment scene at Trotton, Sussex (fig. 17).

19. *Speculum Sacerdotale*, p. 52.

20. J. K. Mozley, "Binding and Loosing," *Encyclopaedia of Religion and Ethics*, ed. James Hastings (rpt. New York: Scribner's, 1958), II, 618-21.

21. Siegfried Wenzel, "The Three Enemies of Man," *Mediaeval Studies*, 29 (1967), 47-66.

22. Ibid.

23. Hugh of St. Victor, *In Ecclesiasten, homilia* 16, as quoted by Wenzel, "Three Enemies of Man," p. 52.

24. Baker and Murphy, "Late Medieval Plays of MS. Digby 133," pp. 162-63; cf. Clifford Davidson, "The Digby *Mary Magdalene* and the Magdalene Cult of the Middle Ages," *Annuale Mediaevale*, 13 (1972), 70-73, and "The Middle English Saint Play," in *The Saint Play in Medieval Europe*, Early Drama, Art, and Music, Monograph Ser., 8

NOTES

(Kalamazoo: Medieval Institute Publications, 1986), pp. 77-78.

25. See stage directions at ll. 304, 333, and 357 in the Digby *Mary Magdalene*.

26. See Adolf Katzenellenbogen, *Allegories of the Virtues and Vices in Mediaeval Art*, trans. Alan J. P. Crick (1939; rpt. New York: Norton, 1964). For a convenient edition of Prudentius' *Psychomachia*, see the Loeb Classical Library edition of this writer's work, with translation by H. J. Thomson (Cambridge: Harvard Univ. Press, 1949), I, 274-343.

27. Arthur Gardner, *English Medieval Sculpture*, revised ed. (1951; rpt. New York: Hacker, 1973), fig. 165; the same plate shows another figure, a man with a toothache, whose reaction to pain is very similar.

28. Cf. Fletcher, "The Meaning of 'Gostly to owr purpos'," pp. 301-02.

29. See Stanley J. Kahrl, *Traditions of Medieval English Drama* (London: Hutchinson, 1974), p. 117.

30. Sandra Billington, however, suggests that Mischief alone would be dressed as a fool ("'Suffer Fools Gladly': The Fool in Medieval England and the Play *Mankind*," in *The Fool and the Trickster: Studies in Honour of Enid Welsford* [Cambridge: D. S. Brewer, 1979], pp. 46-47), but the evidence of the text would seem to me to support only the depiction of Nought in such garb.

31. Remnant, *Catalogue*, p. 154.

32. Ibid., p. 176; see also Bodleian Library MS. Laud. Lat. 114, fol. 71.

33. See *Macro Plays*, ed. Eccles, p. 217.

34. D. J. Gifford, "Iconographical Notes toward a Definition of the Medieval Fool," *Journal of the Warburg and Courtauld Institutes*, 37 (1974), 338.

35. Lucy Freeman Sandler, *The Peterborough Psalter in Brussels and Other Fenland Manuscripts* (London: Harvey Miller, 1974), p. 95.

36. Gifford, "Iconographical Notes," p. 336.

37. Sandler, *Peterborough Psalter*, fig. 41.

38. Ibid., fig. 124; illustration for Psalm 51.

39. Tilley M 805; see additional references in Eccles, ed., *Macro Plays*, p. 219.

40. On this passage, see W. K. Smart, "Some Notes on Mankind," *Modern Philology*, 14 (1916), 294, and Coogan, *An Interpretation*, pp. 29-30, who cites the discussion of fasting in the *Speculum Sacerdotale*, pp. 56-57.

41. For an example of this obscene gesture used elsewhere in drama,

NOTES

see the *Mactacio Abel* ("Com kis myne ars!" [l. 2]) by the Wakefield Master (*The Wakefield Pageants in the Towneley Cycle*, ed. A. C. Cawley [Manchester: Manchester Univ. Press, 1958], p. 2), and, in the visual arts, see Jean Fouquet's famous miniature of the Martyrdom of St. Apollonia (*The Hours of Etienne Chevalier*, introd. and legends by Claude Schaefer [New York: Braziller, 1971], Pl. 45).

42. Remnant, *Catalogue*, p. 98.

43. See ibid., pp. 24, 49; Sally-Beth MacLean, *Chester Art*, Early Drama, Art, and Music, Reference Ser., 3 (Kalamazoo: Medieval Institute Publications, 1982), p. 70.

44. M. D. Anderson, "The Iconography of British Misericords," in Remnant, *Catalogue*, p. xxviii.

45. See Coogan, *An Interpretation*, p. 48, and also Davenport, *Fifteenth-Century English Drama*, pp. 43-44. For a study of the iconography of the spade, see Steven May, "A Medieval Stage Property: The Spade," *Medieval English Theatre*, 4 (1982), 77-92.

46. Caviness, *Early Stained Glass*, fig. 6.

47. Ibid., p. 104.

48. See Remnant, *Catalogue*, p. 18.

49. W. O. Hassall, *The Holkham Bible Picture Book* (London: Dropmore Press, 1954), fol. 4v.

50. Lawrence L. Besserman, *The Legend of Job in the Middle Ages* (Cambridge: Harvard Univ. Press, 1979), p. 111. Southern's comments on this scene are misleading, since he thinks that the paper is the badge which he pins "on his bosom" (*Staging of Plays Before Shakespeare*, pp. 28-29).

51. *Moralia in Job*; see Lorraine Kochanske Stock, "The Thematic and Structural Unity of Mankind," *Studies in Philology*, 72 (1975), 389-90, and Neuss, "Active and Idle Language," pp. 47-49, for comment on Job and *Mankind*.

52. Prudentius, *Psychomachia*, ll. 163ff; see Besserman, *Legend of Job*, p. 70.

53. Ibid., Pls. 17-18; see also Helen Woodruff, *The Illustrated Manuscripts of Prudentius* (Cambridge: Harvard Univ. Press, 1930), figs. 94-95, 97.

54. G. von der Osten, "Job and Christ," *Journal of the Warburg and Courtauld Institutes*, 16 (1953), 155; Louis Réau, *Iconographie de l'art Chrétien* (Paris: Presses Universitaires de France, 1955-59), II, Pt. 1, 317-18. In continental versions of the *Speculum Humanae Salvationis*, Job is frequently shown *in stercore* with his three friends and his wife.

NOTES

Two interesting examples which are useful for this study thus appear in versions of the *Speculum Humanae Salvationis* available on color microfilm in the Hill Monastic Manuscript Library at St. John's University, Collegeville, Minnnesota; these are Codex Admontensis 101, fol. 23, which shows Job's wife pointing her finger at him while behind the group of figures is an unfinished demon, and Codex Cremifanensis 243, fol. 26, which illustrates his wife with a scourge and a devil with a similar implement.

55. See especially Stock, "Thematic and Structural Unity," pp. 389-90.

56. See Réau, *Iconographie*, II, Pt. 1, 315-16.

57. Altarpiece, by the Master of the Legend of St. Barbara; Besserman, *Legend of Job*, Pl. 9.

58. See Clifford Davidson and David E. O'Connor, *York Art*, Early Drama, Art, and Music, Reference Ser., 1 (Kalamazoo: Medieval Institute Publications, 1978), pp. 19-20.

59. Neuss, "Active and Idle Language," pp. 54-55. For a general discussion of the function of scatological iconography, see Karl P. Wentersdorf, "The Symbolic Significance of *Figurae Scatologicae* in Gothic Manuscripts," in *Word, Picture, and Spectacle*, ed. Clifford Davidson, Early Drama, Art, and Music, Monograph Ser., 5 (Kalamazoo: Medieval Institute Publications, 1984), pp. 1-19.

60. Von der Osten, "Job and Christ," pp. 153-58.

61. Walter K. Smart, "Mankind and the Mumming Plays," *Modern Language Notes*, 32 (1917), 21-25. For a study of the role of Titivillus in relation to the themes of the play, see especially Ashley, "Titivillus and the Battle of Words in *Mankind*," pp. 128-50.

61. *Jacob's Well*, ed. Arthur Brandeis, EETS, o.s. 115 (1900), p. 114. See also Margaret Jennings, *Tutivillus: The Literary Career of the Recording Demon*, Studies in Philology, 74, No. 5 (1977), pp. 12-13, 65. For an interesting continental example from an area with close relations to English iconography, see Ebbe Nyborg, *Fanden paa Væggen* (Wormianum, 1978), p. 67.

63. *The Towneley Plays*, ed. George England, EETS, e.s. 71 (1897), p. 375. See also Clifford Davidson, "An Interpretation of the Wakefield Judicium," *Annuale Mediaevale*, 10 (1969), 110-12; Jennings, *Tutivillus*, pp. 58-64.

64. Ibid., p. 60; Ashley, "Titivillus and the Battle of Words," pp. 128-50. See also Clifford Davidson, "Jest and Earnest: Comedy in the Work of the Wakefield Master," *Annuale Mediaevale*, 22 (1982), 81-83.

NOTES

65. M. D. Anderson, *Drama and Imagery in English Medieval Churches* (Cambridge: Cambridge Univ. Press, 1963), pp. 169-70; Remnant, *Catalogue*, p. 19.
66. Robert of Brunne, *Handlyng Synne*, Part II, ed. Frederick J. Furnivall, EETS, o.s. 123 (1902), pp. 290-92.
67. See also Jennings, *Tutivillus*, pp. 27-30.
68. For an example of a black mass in the visual arts, see Tristram, *English Wall Painting of the Fourteenth Century*, pp. 111-12.
69. Stock, "Thematic and Structural Unity," pp. 404-05, citing Rabanus Maurus, *Commentarium in Matthaeum*, IV.
70. At Seething, Norfolk, a small devil steals a set of prayer beads from a pair of women; see Tristram, *English Wall Painting of the Fourteenth Century*, pp. 109, 245.
71. See Christopher Marlowe, *Doctor Faustus*, ed. John Jump (London: Methuen, 1962), pp. 32-33. Faustus is not, of course, married, but rather requests a wife, whereupon the devil offers him "a Devil dressed like a woman" (v.148) to turn his mind away from marriage.
72. Wenzel, *The Sin of Sloth*, p. 151.
73. John Mirk, *Festial*, ed. Theodor Erbe, EETS, e.s. 96 (1905), p. 63; see aso Morton W. Bloomfield, *The Seven Deadly Sins* (East Lansing: Michigan State Univ. Press, 1952); Rosamund Tuve, "Notes on the Virtues and Vices," *Journal of the Warburg and Courtauld Institutes*, 26 (1963), 264-303; 27 (1964), 42-72.
74. John Piggot, Jr., "Notes on the Polychromatic Decoration of Churches, with Special Reference to a Wall Painting Discovered in Ingatestone Church," *Transactions of the Essex Archaeological Society*, 4 (1879), 140 and Pl. facing this page; Tristram, *English Wall Painting of the Fourteenth Century*, p. 186; for another example at Kentford, Suffolk, see ibid., p. 187.
75. Wenzel, *The Sin of Sloth*, p. 152.
76. Karl Young, *The Drama of the Medieval Church* (Oxford: Clarendon Press, 1933), II, 360-64.
77. Émile Mâle, *Religious Art in France: The Twelfth Century*, trans. Marthiel Matthews and ed. Harry Bober, Bollingen Ser., 90, Pt. 1 (Princeton: Princeton Univ. Press, 1978), pp. 198-99. On the phenomenology of right and left and the orientation of depictions of the Last Judgment, see Clifford Davidson, "Space and Time in Medieval Drama: Meditations on Orientation in the Early Theater," in *Word, Picture, and Spectacle*, pp. 40-46.
78. Mâle, *Religious Art in France: The Twelfth Century*, p. 198;

NOTES

Charles Ilsley Minott, *Martin Schongauer* (New York: Collectors Editions, 1971), Pls. 76-86.

79. See Davidson, "The Middle English Saint Play," p. 82.

80. See *Jacob's Well*, pp. 147-48.

81. Neuss, "Active and Idle Language," pp. 63-64.

82. See especially *Apocalypse* 13.8.

83. Statutes at Large, III, 362, as quoted by Smart, "Some Notes on Mankind," pp. 304-05. See also Davenport, *Fifteenth-Century English Drama*, p. 39, who points out an analogy between short jacket and the language characteristic of the vice figures. For a curious continental example of a coat being shortened with a sword, see the version of the *Speculum Humanae Salvationis* in Codex Admontensis 101, fol. 24.

84. Neuss, "Active and Idle Language," pp. 64-65.

85. Francis P. Magoun, Jr., "Football in Medieval England and in Middle-English Literature," *American Historical Review*, 35 (1929-30), 41-42.

86. Ernst Kitzinger, *Early Medieval Art in the British Museum*, 2nd ed. (London: British Museum, 1955), p. 21, Pl. 7.

87. Sandler, *Peterborough Psalter*, figs. 41, 124.

88. *Faerie Queene*, I.ix.50. Despair is also a character in John Skelton's *Magnificence*; see the edition of Paula Neuss (Manchester: Manchester Univ. Press, 1980), pp. 202-04.

89. Susan Snyder, "The Left Hand of God: Despair in Medieval and Renaissance Tradition," *Studies in the Renaissance*, 12 (1965), 18-59.

90. Ibid., p. 55; James H. Stubblebine, *Giotto: The Arena Chapel Frescoes* (New York: Norton, 1969), fig. 57.

91. Snyder, "Left Hand of God," pp. 20-22.

92. H. S. Kingsford, *Illustrations of the Occasional Offices of the Church in the Middle Ages from Contemporary Sources*, Alcuin Club Collections, 24 (London: A. R. Mowbray, 1921), fig. 11.

CHAPTER II:
THE CASTLE OF PERSEVERANCE:
THE ICONOGRAPHY OF ALIENATION
AND RECONCILIATION

1. Milla Riggio, "The Allegory of Feudal Acquisition in *The Castle of Perseverance*," in *Allegory, Myth, and Symbol*, ed. Morton W. Bloom-

NOTES

field, Harvard English Studies, 9 (Cambridge: Harvard Univ. Press, 1981), p. 188. For an important interpretation of the intended function of the manuscript of *The Castle of Perseverance*, see David Parry, "A Margin of Error: The Problem of Marginalia in *The Castle of Perseverance*," in *Editing Early English Drama: Special Problems and New Directions*, ed. A. F. Johnston (New York: AMS Press, 1987), pp. 32-60. Parry speculates that "Perhaps what we now possess is a manuscript copy of the text made for a reader with quite different interests" than theatrical production "by one who had no theatrical or even literary interest in the text whatsoever" (p. 59).

2. See also Clifford Davidson, "Space and Time in Medieval Drama," pp. 44-46. Further reasons for the orientation of the stage in *The Castle of Perseverance* have been suggested by Natalie Crohn Schmitt in her review of the Poculi Ludique Societas/Records of Early English Drama production at Toronto: "Heaven is in the east not only to signify the Holy City of Jerusalem but also to catch the last rays of the sun, for it and the sedes of Greediness to the northeast are heavily used at the end of the play" (*Research Opportunities in Renaissance Drama*, 22 [1979], 144).

3. Cf. M. D. Anderson, *The Imagery of British Churches* (London: John Murray, 1955), pp. 67-68.

4. Beadle, "The Medieval Drama of East Anglia," pp. 166-67.

5. Field Book of the Manors of Walsham-le-Willows and Walsham Churchhouse, fol. 59^v, as quoted by Kenneth M. Dodd, "Another Elizabethan Theater in the Round," *Shakespeare Quarterly*, 21 (1970), 126; see also ibid., pp. 137, 151, and A. C. Cawley, "The Staging of Medieval Drama," in *The Revels History of Drama in English, I: Medieval Drama*, ed. Lois Potter (London: Methuen, 1983), pp. 14-19.

6. Ibid., p. 14, and especially Beadle, "The Medieval Drama of East Anglia," p. 168, for a reference to John Capgrave's *Solace of Pilgrims*, which notes that ancient Roman theaters are similar to the round playing places of East Anglia ("swech as we haue her in this lond").

7. W. Stukeley, *Itinerarium Curiosum* (1776), II, 43; quoted by Cawley, "The Staging of Medieval Drama," p. 15.

8. See the review of the PLS/REED production by Schmitt in *Research Opportunities*, pp. 143-45. On the staging of this play, see also Steven I. Pederson, "The Staging of *The Castle of Perseverance*: A Re-Analysis," *Theatre Notebook*, 39 (1985), 56-57.

9. Arthur Forstater and Joseph L. Baird, "'Walking and Wending': Mankind's Opening Speech," *Theatre Notebook*, 26 (1971-72), 60-64.

10. On pilgrimage in theory and practice, see especially Jonathan

NOTES

Sumption, *Pilgrimage: An Image of Mediaeval Religion* (London: Faber and Faber, 1975), and Victor Turner and Edith Turner, *Image and Pilgrimage in Christian Culture* (New York: Columbia Univ. Press, 1978). For a different view from mine, but one which is strongly and attractively presented, see Edgar Schell, "On the Imitation of Life's Pilgrimage in *The Castle of Perseverance*," in *Medieval English Drama*, ed. Jerome Taylor and Alan H. Nelson (Chicago: Univ. of Chicago Press, 1972), pp. 279-91, and the same author's *Strangers and Pilgrims* (Chicago: Univ. of Chicago Press, 1983), pp. 1-51.

11. See Gerhart B. Ladner, "*Homo Viator*: Mediaeval Ideas on Alienation and Order," *Speculum*, 42 (1967), 233-59.

12. Siegfried Wenzel, "The Pilgrimage of Life as a Late Medieval Genre," *Mediaeval Studies*, 35 (1973), 383.

13. See Sumption, *Pilgrimage, passim*. The proximity of the famous shrine at Walsingham in Norfolk should have made the traditions of pilgrimage familiar to all in East Anglia and other nearby counties.

14. Southern's reconstruction of the stage plan for *The Castle of Perseverance*, first advanced in 1958, is refuted by Natalie Crohn Schmitt, "Was There a Medieval Theatre in the Round? A Re-examination of the Evidence," in *Medieval English Drama*, ed. Taylor and Nelson, pp. 292-315. See also William Tydeman, *The Theatre in the Middle Ages* (Cambridge: Cambridge Univ. Press, 1978), pp. 156-59.

15. See Davidson, "Space and Time in Medieval Drama," pp. 44-46, and Beadle, "The Medieval Drama of East Anglia," pp. 168ff.

16. The most controversial aspect of Southern's reconstruction is his placement of the ditch; for the solution arrived at for the Toronto production, see the review in *Research Opportunities* by Schmitt, p. 143.

17. Alan H. Nelson, "'Of the seuen ages': An Unknown Analogue of *The Castle of Perseverance*," *Comparative Drama*, 8 (1974), 125-38; cf. Samuel C. Chew, *The Pilgrimage of Life* (New York: Yale Univ. Press, 1962), pp. 163-69. For a full study of the Ages of Man *topos*, see Elizabeth Sears, *The Ages of Man* (Princeton: Princeton Univ. Press, 1986).

18. See also Nelson, "'Of the seuen ages'," pp. 130, 133.

19. See also ibid., p. 130, 133.

20. See Creighton Gilbert, "When Did a Man in the Renaissance Grow Old?" *Studies in the Renaissance*, 14 (1967), 7-32.

21. Nelson, "'Of the seuen ages'," p. 128.

22. See ibid., p. 126.

23. Audrey Baker, "The Interpretation and Iconography of the Long-

NOTES

thorpe Paintings," *Archaeologia*, 96 (1955), 43-44; E. Clive Rouse, "The Wall Paintings at Longthorpe Tower Near Peterborough, Northants," *Archaeologia*, 96 (1955), Pls. VII, XV, XVI.

24. Souls are commonly received from the dying body by the appropriate figure, either an angel or a devil. In the visual arts, therefore, angels are normally shown taking souls up to heaven; see, for example, the wall paintings at Northmoor, near Oxford, and Winchelsea, Sussex (Tristram, *English Wall Painting in the Fourteenth Century*, pp. 229, 266). See also fn. 27, below, for an example of the receipt of a damned soul, and additionally Fritz Saxl, "A Spiritual Encyclopaedia of the Later Middle Ages," *Journal of the Warburg and Courtauld Institutes*, 5 (1942), 95-96.

25. See Nelson, "'Of the seuen ages'," p. 126, 132.

26. See also ibid., p. 135.

27. *Inventory of the Historical Monuments in the City of York*, IV (London: HMSO, 1975), Pl. 29a.

28. *Phaedo* 108B; *The Collected Dialogues of Plato*, ed. Edith Hamilton and Huntington Cairns, Bollingen Ser., 71 (Princeton: Princeton Univ. Press, 1961), p. 89.

29. *Oxford Dictionary of the Christian Church*, p. 606.

30. *His Commands* II.vi.2; *The Apostolic Fathers*, introd. W. Burton (London: Griffith, Farran, Okeden, and Welsh, n.d.), I, 238.

31. Ibid., I, 238-39.

32. See especially St. Augustine's *City of God* XIV.13.

33. Piggot, "Notes," facing p. 140; Tristram, *English Wall Painting of the Fourteenth Century*, p. 185. It should be noted, however, that the Virtues are also associated with the higher level, in this case the upper level of the castle; see Pederson, "The Staging," p. 106.

34. On the possible disappearance of these two characters after l. 790, see Southern, *Medieval Theatre in the Round*, p. 196.

35. See Clifford Davidson, "The Iconography of Wisdom and Folly in *King Lear*," in *Shakespeare and the Emblem: Studies in Renaissance Iconography and Iconology*, ed. Tibor Fabiny, Papers in English and American Studies, 3 (Szeged, Hungary: Department of English, Attila József Univ., 1984), pp. 189-214.

36. The Renaissance writer Ben Jonson calls attention to this practice in his *Masque of Queens* when he describes the witches who dance therein: "*at their meetings* [they] *do all things contrary to the custom of men, dancing back to back and hip to hip, their hands joined, and making their circles backward, to the left hand* . . ." (*Selected Masques*, ed.

NOTES

Stephen Orgel [New Haven: Yale Univ. Press, 1970], p. 92).

37. See Chapter I, above, and fig. 17, which shows the Seven Deadly Sins at Trotton (described by Tristram, *English Wall Painting of the Fourteenth Century*, p. 259).

38. St. Basil, *Exegetic Homilies*, trans. Agnes Clare Way (Washington: Catholic Univ. of America Press, 1963), pp. 257-58. See also *Oxford Dictionary of the Christian Church*, p. 606, for summary of views.

39. See Thomas N. Tentler, *Sin and Confession on the Eve of the Reformation* (Princeton: Princeton Univ. Press, 1977), pp. 109-11.

40. See, for example, Kingsford, *Illustrations of the Occasional Offices*, figs. 6, 11-15, 44.

41. Tentler, *Sin and Confession*, pp. 67-68.

42. Davidson, "The Middle English Saint Play," p. 79-80.

43. Schmitt, "Was There a Medieval Theatre in the Round?" p. 299.

44. Merle Fifield, "The Arena Theatres in Vienna Codices 2535 and 2536," *Comparative Drama*, 2 (1968-69), 259-82, and "The French Manuscripts of *La Forteresse de la Foy*," *Manuscripta*, 16 (1972), 98-111.

45. Fifield, "The Arena Theatres," Pls. 3, 7.

46. Southern, *Medieval Theatre in the Round*, figs. 19-20, 22.

47. Charles Read Baskerville, "Dramatic Aspects of Medieval Folk Festivals in England," *Studies in Philology*, 17 (1920), 57-60; attention is called to this article by Potter, *English Morality Play*, p. 13.

48. *Macro Plays*, ed. Bevington, p. xviii.

49. For the latter, see Herrad of Landsberg, *Hortus Deliciarum*, Pls. XLIII-LI, XXXVIII.

50. See the cautions expressed by Rosalie B. Green, "Virtues and Vices in the Chapter House Vestibule in Salisbury," *Journal of the Warburg and Courtauld Institutes*, 31 (1968), 150.

51. Ibid., Pl. 54.

52. Ibid., Pl. 58a.

53. Émile Mâle, *Religious Art in France: The Thirteenth Century*, trans. Marthiel Matthews and ed. Harry Bober, Bollingen Ser., 90, Pt. 2 (Princeton: Princeton Univ. Press, 1984), fig. 72, pp. 117-18.

54. Folke Nordström, *Virtues and Vices on the 14th Century Corbels in the Choir of Uppsala Cathedral* (Stockholm: Almqvist & Wiksell, 1956), p. 63.

55. See George Ferguson, *Signs and Symbols in Christian Art* (1954; rpt. New York: Oxford Univ. Press, 1961), p. 23. It is not surprising that

NOTES

the pelican was a popular figure often carved on misericords; see Remnant, *Catalogue*, Pl. 12, and *passim*. In the De Lisle Psalter (British Library Arundel MS. 83), the pelican is placed at the top of the Tree of Life (fol. 125ᵛ); see Lucy Freeman Sandler, *The Psalter of Robert de Lisle in the British Library* (London: Harvey Miller, 1983), fig. 49.

56. Katzenellenbogen, *Allegories of the Virtues and Vices*, p. 63.

57. Ibid., Pls. 64-65; see also the commentary in Saxl, "A Spiritual Encyclopaedia," pp. 118-19.

58. See also Sandler, *The Psalter of Robert de Lisle*, Pl. 8.

59. Mâle, *Religious Art in France: The Thirteenth Century*, p. 123.

60. Roberta D. Cornelius, *The Figurative Castle* (Bryn Mawr, 1930).

61. *Apostolic Fathers*, I, 223.

62. Hans Achelis, *Die Katakomben von Neapel* (Leipzig, 1936), Pl. 10.

63. Hildegard of Bingen, *Liber Scivias*, ed. Adelgundis Führkötter (Turnhout: Brepols, 1978), II, Pl. facing p. 516. See also Katzenellenbogen, *Allegories of the Virtues and Vices*, pp. 42-43.

64. Cornelius, *Figurative Castle*, pp. 27-32; *Sawles Warde*, ed. Richard Morris, EETS, o.s. 34 (1868), pp. 245ff; for a study of the Castle of Virtue as a sermon commonplace, see G. R. Owst, *Literature and Pulpit in Medieval England*, 2nd ed. (Oxford: Basil Blackwell, 1961), pp. 77-85.

65. Rosemary Woolf, "The Theme of Christ the Lover-Knight in Medieval English Literature," *Review of English Studies*, n.s. 13 (1962), 1-16.

66. See Eric George Millar, *The Luttrell Psalter* (London: British Museum, 1932), pp. 31-32; cf. Roger Sherman Loomis, "The Allegorical Siege in the Art of the Middle Ages," *American Journal of Archaeology*, n.s. 23 (1919), 259-61, for a secular interpretation. For commentary on the mirror case in the Victoria and Albert Museum as well as on other examples of mirror cases with the Castle of Love, see Margaret H. Longhurst, *Catalogue of Carvings in Ivory*, Part II (London: Victoria and Albert Museum, 1929), pp. 48-49, Pl. XLIV. For another interesting example, see William R. Levin et al., *Images of Love and Death in Late Medieval and Renaissance Art* (Ann Arbor: Univ. of Michigan Museum of Art, 1976), pp. 106-08.

67. Sandler, *Peterborough Psalter*, fig. 57. Cf. Loomis, p. 259; but see Merle Fifield, "The Assault on the *Castle of Perseverance*--The Tradition and the Figure," *Ball State University Forum*, 16, No. 4 (Autumn 1975), 23.

NOTES

68. The bear as a symbol could be ambiguous, to be sure, since the bestiary explanation tended to emphasize fabulous characteristics of a positive nature. The negative understanding of the bear remains, particularly in its sexual sense, in as late a work as Sidney's *Arcadia (The Prose Works*, ed. Albert Feuillerat [1912; rpt. Cambridge: Cambridge Univ. Press, 1963], IV, 47ff).

69. Loomis, to be sure, also cites an "ecclesiastical version of the Siege motif" (p. 264, fig. 7).

70. Katzenellenbogen, *Allegories of the Virtues and Vices*, fig. 15.

71. Green, "Virtues and Vices in the Chapter House Vestibule at Salisbury," Pl. 52c.

72. Ibid., p. 152.

73. Tristram, *English Wall Painting of the Fourteenth Century*, p. 183.

74. Ibid., p. 259; A. Caiger-Smith, *English Medieval Mural Paintings* (Oxford: Clarendon Press, 1963), Pl. XVIII.

75. Ibid., Pl. XVIII; Tristram, *English Wall Painting of the Fourteenth Century*, pp. 259-60.

76. Cf. *Virtues and Vices*, ed. F. Holthausen, EETS, o.s. 89 (1888), pp. 10-11; I. B. Cauthen, Jr., "'The Foule Flibbertigibbet'--'King Lear,' III.iv.113, IV.i.60," *Notes and Queries*, 206 (1958), 98-99.

77. See Kenneth Varty, *Reynard the Fox: A Study of the Fox in Medieval English Art* (New York: Humanities Press, 1967), *passim*. Backbiter additionally may share with the World the distinction of being *literally* fair before and foul behind, as in the case of the sculpture of the Prince of This World at Strasbourg Cathedral. See R. M. Frye, *The Renaissance* Hamlet (Princeton: Princeton Univ. Press, 1984), pp. 227-29, fig. VI.15.

78. On the playing of these scenes, see Southern, *Medieval Theatre in the Round*, pp. 193-94.

79. See Thomas Sharp, *A Dissertation*, Pl. 6, showing a detail of the Stratford-upon-Avon wall painting of the Doom with devils blowing horns, and Pierre Turpin, "Devils Blowing Horns or Trumpets," *Notes and Queries*, 12th ser., 5 (1919), 186-87. In Greek mythology, the moral superiority of string music over wind music is asserted by the stories of the contests of Apollo with Marsyas and Pan; see the convenient summary of these contests in Robert Graves, *Greek Myths*, 2nd ed. (Harmondsworth: Penguin, 1960), I, 77.

80. *Macro Plays*, ed. Eccles, p. 1. On the stage action involved, see Philip Butterworth, "Gunnepowdyr, Fyre and Thondyr," *Medieval English*

NOTES

Theatre, 7 (1985), 68-76.

81. Ibid., p. 195; Anderson, *Drama and Imagery*, p. 81; Ferguson, *Signs and Symbols*, pp. 37-38; and Saxl, "Spiritual Encyclopaedia," p. 104.

82. Anderson, *Drama and Imagery*, Pl. 1a; Francis Bond, *Fonts and Font Covers* (London: Oxford Univ. Press, 1908), pp. 176, 181.

83. The importance of avarice in the play has been stressed by J. Wilson McCutchan, "Covetousness in *The Castle of Perseverance*," in *English Studies in Honor of James Southall Wilson*, Univ. of Virginia Studies, 4 (Charlottesville, 1951), pp. 175-91. Concern with this vice in particular should not be surprising since, as Lester K. Little points out, it became the focus of attention in the later Middle Ages ("Pride Goes before Avarice: Social Change and Vices in Latin Christendom," *American Historical Review*, 76 [1971], 16-49).

84. *Macro Plays*, ed. Bevington, p. 152; ed. Eccles, p. 1.

85. Southern, *Medieval Theatre in the Round*, p. 205.

86. Schmitt, "Was There a Medieval Theatre in the Round?" fig. 21; see also Walter S. Gibson, *Hieronymus Bosch* (New York and Washington: Praeger, 1973), pp. 46-47, fig. 32, and especially Alan J. Fletcher, "Coveytyse Copbord schal be at the Ende of the Castel be the Beddys Feet," *English Studies*, 68 (1987), 305-12.

87. Anderson, *Drama and Imagery*, Pl. 24c.

88. Tristram, *English Wall Painting of the Fourteenth Century*, p. 259.

89. Ibid., pp. 137, 160; De Lisle Psalter, fol. 128^v, which shows an avaricious man holding a money bag while a devil appears behind him; in contrast, this illumination shows the good man in prayer--a pose that renders him safe against the devil. See Sandler, *The Psalter of Robert de Lisle*, Pl. 8.

90. Tristram, *English Wall Painting of the Fourteenth Century*, p. 183. See also David Bevington, "'Man, thinke on thine endinge day': Stage Pictures of Just Judgment in *The Castle of Perseverance*," in *Homo, Memento Finis*, Early Drama, Art, and Music, Monograph Ser., 6 (Kalamazoo: Medieval Institute Publications, 1985), p. 160.

91. See also Gail McMurray Gibson, "East Anglian Drama and the Dance of Death: Some Second Thoughts on the 'Dance of Paul's'," *EDAM Newsletter*, 5, No. 1 (Fall 1982), 1-9. For a fuller discussion of the Dance of Death motif, see below, Chapter IV.

92. Riggio, "The Allegory of Feudal Acquisition," p. 203; cf. Little, "Pride Goes Before Avarice," pp. 16-49.

NOTES

93. Humanum Genus comments: "Certis a vers that Dauid spak/ I the sawter I fynde it trewe:/ Tesaurizat et ignorat cui congregabit ea./ Tresor, tresor, it hathe no tak;/ It is othyr mens, olde and newe" (ll. 2984-88).

94. Riggio, "The Allegory of Feudal Acquisition," pp. 203-04.

95. Cf. Gibson, *Hieronymus Bosch*, pp. 46-47.

96. See T. S. R. Boase, *Death in the Middle Ages* (London: Thames and Hudson, 1972), pp. 119-24; Philippe Ariès, *The Hour of Our Death*, trans. Helen Weaver (New York: Knopf, 1981), pp. 105-09.

97. Ibid., pp. 5-10.

98. Kingsford, *Illustrations of the Occasional Offices*, fig. 28.

99. Ibid., figs. 30-31.

100. *Macro Plays*, ed. Eccles, p. 1; ed. Bevington, p. 152.

101. See also Nelson, "'Of the seuen ages'," p. 135.

102. See, for example, the twelfth-century sculpture now at York Minster which illustrates a cauldron with souls of the damned over a fire and devils attending the scene (Edward S. Prior and Arthur Gardner, *An Account of Medieval Figure-Sculpture in England* [Cambridge: Cambridge Univ. Press, 1912], fig. 192).

103. See, for example, Sharp, *Dissertation*, pp. 56-57.

104. Hilary Wayment, *The Stained Glass of the Church of St. Mary, Fairford, Gloucestershire* (London: Society of Antiquaries, 1984), p. 55, Pl. 22; Oscar Farmer, *Fairford Church and Its Stained Glass Windows*, 8th ed. (Bath, 1968), p. 30. On the glass before restoration, see also H. H. J. Westlake, *A History of Design in Painted Glass* (1881-94), III, 104-05, but see also Hilary Wayment, "'Echo answers where': The Victorian 'Restoration' of the Great West Window at Fairford," *Journal of the British Society of Master Glass Painters*, 17 (1980-81), 18-27.

105. *Meditations on the Life of Christ*, trans. Isa Ragusa and Rosalie B. Green (Princeton: Princeton Univ. Press, 1961), pp. 6-9. On the Four Daughters of God, see also Hope Traver, *The Four Daughters of God* (Philadelphia: John C. Winston, 1907), and Samuel C. Chew, *The Virtues Reconciled* (Toronto: Univ. of Toronto Press, 1947).

106. *Ludus Coventriae*, pp. 97-104. For another treatment of the Four Daughters of God in drama of the fifteenth century from England, see the third act of Chaundler's *Liber Apologeticus*, ed. Shoukri, pp. 106-39. For a valuable comparative study, see Sarah Carpenter, "From God to Man: The Development of the Parliament of Heaven in English Drama," in *Atti del IV Colloquio della Société Internationale pour l'Etude du Théâtre Médiévale*, ed. M. Chiabò, F. Doglio, and M. Maymone (Viterbo: Centro Studi sul Teatro Medioevale e Rinascimentale, [1984]), pp. 600-02.

107. *The Minor Poems of the Vernon MS.*, ed. Carl Horstmann, EETS, o.s. 98 (1892), pp. 355-94, esp. 362-69.
108. *Macro Plays*, ed. Eccles, p. 1.
109. Ibid., p. 1.
110. Ibid., p. 1.
111. Ibid., p. 1.
112. Chew, *Virtues Reconciled*, Pl. 1.
113. Ibid., Pl. 3; see also Pls. 2, 4-5.
114. JoAnna Dutka, *Music in the English Mystery Plays*, Early Drama, Art, and Music, Reference Ser., 2 (Kalamazoo: Medieval Institute Publications, 1980), p. 42.

CHAPTER III:
WISDOM: THE ICONOGRAPHY OF MYSTICISM

1. Gibson, "The Play of Wisdom and the Abbey of St. Edmund," pp. 126, 130. For another view, see Alexandra F. Johnston, "*Wisdom* and the Records: Is There a Moral?" in *The* Wisdom *Symposium*, ed. Riggio, pp. 87-102. Johnston suggests the possibility of the production of *Wisdom* in a great household such as that maintained by "a serious-minded local magnate who was prepared to pay for lavish entertainments" (p. 96).
2. *Research Opportunities in Renaissance Drama*, 24 (1981), 197.
3. Bevington, "'Blake and wyght, fowll and fayer'," p. 137.
4. Davenport, *Fifteenth-Century English Drama*, pp. 79, 91.
5. Ibid., p. 79.
6. Davidson and O'Connor, *York Art*, p. 17. The mask worn by Wisdom receives attention in Meg Twycross and Sarah Carpenter, "Masks in Medieval English Theatre: The Mystery Plays," *Medieval English Theatre*, 3 (1981), 19.
7. Francis W. Cheetham, *Medieval English Alabaster Carvings in the Castle Museum, Nottingham*, revised ed. (Nottingham: City of Nottingham Art Galleries and Museum Committee, 1973), p. 39.
8. For the glass at Holy Trinity, Goodramgate, see Davidson and O'Connor, *York Art*, p. 109, fig. 32; the present faces are replacements.
9. Caiger-Smith, *English Medieval Mural Paintings*, Pl. III; E. W. Tristram, *English Medieval Wall Painting: The Twelfth Century* (Oxford: Oxford Univ. Press, 1944), Pl. 3. For other early examples, see ibid., Pl. 75, and E. W. Tristram, *English Medieval Wall Painting: The Thirteenth Century* (Oxford: Oxford Univ. Press, 1950), Pls. 33, 118.

10. Rickert, *Painting in Britain: The Middle Ages*, Pl. 139.

11. See Clement F. Pitman, "Reflections on Nottingham Alabaster Carving," *The Connoisseur*, 133 (1954), 222, fig. x; this example of the Christ in Majesty is now in the Stieglitz Museum, U.S.S.R. For a French woodcut illustrating Christ in Majesty in the lid of a missal box dated c.1481, see Karl Kup, "Notes on a Fifteenth-Century Cofferet," *The Connoisseur*, 140 (1957), fig. 3.

12. John Phillips, *The Reformation of Images* (Berkeley and Los Angeles: Univ. of California Press, 1973), *passim*.

13. Gervase Mathew, *Byzantine Aesthetics* (New York: Viking Press, 1963), p. 97; quotation from the treatise by Porphyry on Images, in the third book of Eusebius of Caesaria, *Praeparatio Evangelia*.

14. Sixten Ringbom, "Devotional Images and Imaginative Devotions," *Gazette des Beaux-Arts*, 111 (1969), 159-70; Theresa Coletti, "Spirituality and Devotional Images: The Staging of the Hegge Cycle," unpubl. Ph.D. diss. (Univ. of Rochester, 1975).

15. Mathew, *Byzantine Aesthetics*, p. 117.

16. Léonide Ouspensky, *Theology of the Icon*, trans. Elizabeth Meyendorff (Crestwood, N.Y.: St. Vladimir's Seminary Press, 1978), p. 160; see also Ernst Kitzinger, "The Cult of Images in the Age before Iconoclasm," *Dumbarton Oaks Papers*, 8 (1954), 121.

17. Ouspensky, *Theology of the Icon*, pp. 160-61.

18. See Clifford Davidson, *From Creation to Doom: The York Cycle of Mystery Plays* (New York: AMS Press, 1984), pp. 131-32; F. M. Salter, *Mediaeval Drama in Chester* (Toronto: Univ. of Toronto Press, 1955), p. 39.

19. See, for example, Turner and Turner, *Image and Pilgrimage in Christian Culture*, pp. 1-39.

20. It is well known that representations of the Father in human form and even of the Holy Spirit in the form of a man were common in the later Middle Ages. On the representation of the Trinity in the theater, see Lynette Muir, "The Trinity in Medieval Drama," in *Drama in the Middle Ages*, ed. Davidson, Gianakaris, and Stroupe, pp. 75-88; but see also the iconographic study of Adelheid Heimann, "Trinitas Creator Mundi," *Journal of the Warburg and Courtauld Institutes*, 2 (1938-39), 42-52.

21. Joseph Coleman Green, *The Medieval Morality of* Wisdom Who Is Christ (Nashville, Tenn., 1938), pp. 1-39; the connection of the figure of Wisdom with the iconography of the Throne of Solomon has been established by Milla Riggio in a paper entitled "The Throne of Wisdom," read at the International Congress on Medieval Studies in Kalamazoo in

NOTES

1985.

22. Smart, *Some English and Latin Sources and Parallels*, pp. 9-38; Eccles, ed., *Macro Plays*, p. xxxiii.

23. See *John* 1.5.

24. Caiger-Smith, *English Medieval Mural Paintings*, Pl. III; cf. Ouspensky, pp. 204-05.

25. Carleton Brown, ed., *Religious Lyrics of the Fifteenth Century* (Oxford: Clarendon Press, 1939), pp. 151-62, and *Religious Lyrics of the XIVth Century*, 2nd ed. (Oxford: Clarendon Press, 1924), pp. 225-28.

26. Otto Pächt and J. J. G. Alexander, *Illuminated Manuscripts in the Bodleian Library, Oxford*, III: *British, Irish, and Icelandic Schools* (Oxford: Clarendon Press, 1973), Pl. LXXVI, fig. 794a. Wounds of this type are not shown in the illustration of Christ as Wisdom (*Weishait*) in an illumination in a German manuscript containing the writings of Henry Suso from 1473; see *The* Wisdom *Colloquium*, ed. Riggio, Pl. facing p. 34.

27. Gertrud Schiller, *Iconography of Christian Art*, trans. Janet Seligman (Greenwich, Conn.: New York Graphic Soc., 1972), II, figs. 681-766.

28. See Riehle, *The Middle English Mystics*, pp. 34-55.

29. See Williams, *Drama of Medieval England*, pp. 157-58. For an example of the *Sponsus* and *Sponsa* in iconography, see the East Anglian Ramsay Psalter (Monastery of St. Paul in the Lavanttal, Carinthia, MS. XXV.2.19, fol. 17; color microfilm available in the Hill Monastic Manuscript Library), which has been dated c.1300; the *Sponsa* is placed at his right hand, and both are crowned. In attendance are St. John the Baptist at the right with the Agnus Dei, and St. John the Evangelist at the left with a book.

The concept of "Christ as lover of the soul" which is central not only to Western Christianity but also to the play of *Wisdom* is noted by Coletti and Sheingorn, "Playing *Wisdom* at Trinity College," p. 179.

30. The *Wisdom* playwright's source is Walter Hilton's *The Scale of Perfection*; see Eccles, ed., *Macro Plays*, p. 205.

31. Book II, i, 1; *The Scale (or Ladder) of Perfection*, ed. Dom Serenus Cressy (Westminster: Art and Book Co., 1908), p. 133. See also Bevington, "'Blake and wyght, fowll and fayer'," pp. 136-37.

32. Quoted by Eccles, ed., *Macro Plays*, p. 205; Hilton, *Scale*, ed. Cressy, p. 144.

33. Summarized by G. Florovsky, *Vizantiiskie otssy V-VIII vekov* (Paris, 1933), p. 173, as quoted in translation by Ouspensky, *Theology of*

NOTES

Theology of the Eastern Church (Cambridge and London: James Clarke, 1957), pp. 114-34.

34. "The Trinitarian Allegory of the Moral Play of *Wisdom*," pp. 121-35; cf. Riehle, pp. 142-50.

35. *On the Trinity*, VI, vi, 12; *A Select Library of the Nicene and Post-Nicene Fathers*, ed. Philip Schaff (rpt. Grand Rapids, Mich.: Eerdmans, 1956), III, 113.

36. Hill, "The Trinitarian Allegory," p. 133; Bernard of Clairvaux, *On the Song of Songs*, 82.

37. Augustine's *memoria, intellegentia,* and *voluntas* are the source of *Mind, Understanding,* and *Will*; cf. Riehle, p. 143.

38. Panofsky, *Early Netherlandish Painting*, II, fig. 284.

39. See ibid., I, 134.

40. Eccles, ed., *Macro Plays*, p. xxxvi.

41. Bernard Spivack, *Shakespeare and the Allegory of Evil* (New York: Columbia Univ. Press, 1958), p. 93.

42. Ibid., p. 93.

43. Schmitt, "The Idea of a Person in Medieval Morality Plays," p. 29.

44. See Hill, "The Trinitarian Allegory," pp. 126-27.

45. On the senses, see Smart, *Some English and Latin Sources and Parallels*, p. 42, and Green, *Medieval Morality of* Wisdom, pp. 90-91, as well as *Jacob's Well*, pp. 222-23; cf. John J. Molloy, *A Theological Interpretation of the Moral Play,* Wisdom Who Is Christ (Washington, D.C.: Catholic Univ. of America Press, 1952), p. 29.

46. See *Matthew* 25.1-13; Mâle, *Religious Art in France: The Thirteenth Century*, pp. 202-03. For an example of the iconography of the Wise and Foolish Virgins, see fig. 10.

47. See Clifford Davidson, "On the Uses of Iconographic Study: The Example of the *Sponsus* from St. Martial of Limoges," *Comparative Drama*, 13 (1979-80), 308; rpt. in *Drama in the Middle Ages*, ed. Davidson, Gianakaris, and Stroupe, pp. 51-52.

48. *Sarum Missal,* ed. Legg, p. 173.

49. *Jacob's Well*, pp. 216-19.

50. Tristram, *English Wall Painting of the Fourteenth Century*, p. 220, Pl. 64b; Rouse, "The Wall Paintings at Longthorpe Tower," Pl. XVII; Baker, "Interpretation and Iconography," pp. 44-47.

51. Around the wheel in this illumination are represented the Ages of Man from childhood to tomb. A variation of this design also appears in the same manuscript on fol. 126; see Sandler, *Psalter of Robert de Lisle*,

NOTES

the same manuscript on fol. 126; see Sandler, *Psalter of Robert de Lisle*, Pl. 3. See also Gordon McN. Rushforth, "The Wheel of the Ten Ages of Life in Leominster Church," *Proceedings of the Society of Antiquaries* (1914), pp. 47-60.

52. *De Genesi ad litteram libri duodecim*, XI, xv, 20, as quoted by Erich Przywara, *An Augustine Synthesis* (New York: Harper and Row, 1958), p. 266.

53. See Esther Casier Quinn, *The Quest of Seth for the Oil of Mercy* (Chicago: Univ. of Chicago Press, 1962); Charles Mills Gayley, *Plays of Our Forefathers* (London: Chatto and Windus, 1908), pp. 246-71.

54. G. McN. Rushforth, "The Windows of the Church of St. Neot, Cornwall," *Exeter Diocesan Architectural and Archaeological Society Journal*, 15 (1937), 157-58, Pl. XXXIX.

55. See above for discussion of this point.

56. Hill, "The Trinitarian Allegory," p. 128.

57. See the edition edited by John D. Jump, p. 19. This edition reprints as frontispiece the title page of the quarto of 1624 which illustrates the devil appearing to Faustus in his own hideous shape at the conjurer's *left*.

58. Milton McC. Gatch, "Mysticism and Satire in the Morality of Wisdom," *Modern Philology*, 73 (1975), 351.

59. Tilley C414.

60. See David Bevington, *Tudor Drama and Politics* (Cambridge: Harvard Univ. Press, 1968), pp. 28-34.

61. See Turpin, "Devils Blowing Horns or Trumpets," pp. 186-87, and Sharp, *Dissertation*, Pl. 6.

62. Lecoy de la Marche, *La chaire française au moyen âge* (Paris, 1886), p. 447, as quoted by Richard Axton, *European Drama of the Early Middle Ages* (London: Hutchinson, 1974), p. 49. On the devil's dance, cf. David L. Jeffrey, "Franciscan Spirituality and the Rise of the Early English Drama," *Mosaic*, 8, No. 4 (1975), 26-27. The tradition that there is something demonic about the ring dance or at least about the folk fiddler who plays for it is still to be found in Sweden, where a particularly inspired fiddler may be called "bockfot"--i.e., goat's, or devil's, foot. On the importance of the dances, see Peter Happé's review of the Winchester production of *Wisdom* in *Research Opportunities* for 1981 (p. 196).

63. See also Eccles, ed., *Macro Plays*, p. 212.

64. Davidson, "The Digby *Mary Magdalene*," p. 78, and "The Middle English Saint Play," p. 83; Colin Slim, "Mary Magdalene, Musician and Dancer," *Early Music*, 8 (1980), 460-73. In British Library Add. MS.

NOTES

24,199, fol. 18, Luxuria dances to music being made by musicians with a lyre and double pipe; this line drawing illustrates the text of Prudentius' *Psychomachia.*

65. Note the pun on 'spendys' in l. 801; for meaning, see the apt definition in Eric Partridge, *Shakespeare's Bawdy,* revised ed. (New York: Dutton, 1969), p. 187.

66. See Chapter IV, below.

67. *Religious Lyrics of the XIVth Century,* ed. Brown, p. 3; cf. St. Augustine, *Confessions,* VIII, v.

68. David Parry, *Households of God: The Rule of St. Benedict with Explanations for Monks and Lay-people Today* (London: Darton, Longman, and Todd, 1980), p. 89.

69. The manuscript calls for "vj small boys in the lyknes of dewyllys" (*Macro Plays,* ed. Bevington, pp. 230-31); Eccles emends the number to "seven small boys" (*s.d.* at l. 912).

70. See Davidson, "The Digby *Mary Magdalene,*" pp. 71, 81.

71. *The City of God,* trans. Marcus Dods *et al.* (New York: Random House, 1950), p. 445 (Book XIV, iv, 1). For an interesting comparison of the disfigured Anima in *Wisdom* to the fallen Soul in Hildegard of Bingen's *Ordo Virtutum,* see Robert Potter, "The *Ordo Virtutum*: Ancestor of the English Moralities?" *Comparative Drama,* 20 (1986), 207-08.

72. See the discussion of this point above.

73. Molloy, *Theological Interpretation,* p. 150; Christopher Wordsworth, *Ceremonies and Processions of the Cathedral Church of Salisbury* (Cambridge: Cambridge Univ. Press, 1901), pp. 68-71.

74. These are from the *Novem Virtutes* formerly attributed to Richard Rolle; see Smart, *Some English and Latin Sources and Parallels,* pp. 34-36.

75. Adolf Katzenellenbogen quotes from the *Glossa Ordinaria*: "As they are called bridegroom and bride, so also head and body. Whether one says, therefore, head and body or bridegroom and bride, understand them as just one. For out of two becomes one person, as it were, namely out of head and body, out of bridegroom and bride" (*The Sculptural Programs of Chartres Cathedral* [1959; rpt. New York: Norton, n.d.], p. 69).

76. Bond, *Fonts and Font Covers,* pp. 176, 181.

77. Davidson and O'Connor, *York Art,* p. 182; Joseph Halfpenny, *Gothic Ornaments in the Cathedral Church of York* (York, 1795), Pl. 95.

78. O. Elfrida Saunders, *English Illumination* (1933; rpt. New York: Hacker, 1969), Pl. 88b. In the continental *Biblia Pauperum,* Ecclesia and

Synagoga may appear in the Crucifixion scene; see, for example, Codex Cremifanensis 328, fol. 6ᵛ, which shows Synagoga blindfolded and seated on an ass that is stumbing (color microfilm in Hill Monastic Microfilm Library). For a study of this iconography, see Charles Singer, "Allegorical Representation of the Synagogue in a Twelfth Century Illuminated MS. of Hildegard of Bingen," *Jewish Quarterly Review*, n.s. 5 (1915), 267-88, and Lewis Edward, "Some English Examples of the Mediaeval Representation of Church and Synagogue," *Transactions of the Jewish Historical Society of England*, 18 (1958), 63-75.

79. Panofsky, *Early Netherlandish Painting*, II, fig. 236.

80. Ibid., I, 145, citing Honorius of Autun, *Commentary on the Song of Songs*.

81. Molloy, *Theological Interpretation*, p. 157.

82. See also M. R. James, *Suffolk and Norfolk* (London: J. M. Dent and Sons, 1930), pp. 107-08.

83. See Eccles, ed., *Macro Plays*, p. 216.

84. *The Book of Margery Kempe*, ed. Sanford Brown Meech, EETS, o.s. 212 (1940), I, 70.

85. Riehle, *Middle English Mystics*, p. 46.

CHAPTER IV:
LIFE'S TERMINUS AND THE MORALITY DRAMA

1. Part II, ll. 10-11; Henry Medwall, *The Plays*, ed. Alan H. Nelson (Cambridge: D. S. Brewer, 1980), p. 127.

2. J. D. Chambers, Population, *Economy, and Society in Pre-Industrial England*, ed. W. A. Armstrong (London: Oxford Univ. Press, 1972), pp. 19-20; *The Pursuit of Holiness in Late Medieval and Renaissance Religion*, ed. Charles Trinkhaus and Heiko A. Oberman (Leiden: Brill, 1974), *passim*; Robert S. Gottfried, *Epidemic Disease in Fifteenth-Century England* (New Brunswick, N.J.: Rutgers Univ. Press, 1978).

3. Tentler, *Sin and Confession*, pp. 57-70.

4. See W. A. Pantin, *The English Church in the Fourteenth Century* (Cambridge: Cambridge Univ. Press, 1955), pp. 189ff.

5. *The English Works of Sir Thomas More*, ed. W. E. Campbell *et al.*, I (London and New York, 1931), 77, as quoted in Farnham, *The Medieval Heritage of Elizabethan Tragedy*, p. 181.

6. Potter, *English Morality Play*, p. 7.

7. G. R. Owst, *Preaching in Medieval England* (1926; rpt. New York:

NOTES

Russell and Russell, 1965), pp. 265-68, 340-44.

8. J. Huizinga, *The Waning of the Middle Ages* (1949; rpt. Garden City, N.Y.: Doubleday, 1954), p. 138.

9. See Émile Mâle, *Religious Art in France: The Late Middle Ages*, pp. 81-135. But see also the discussion in Philippa Tristram, *Figures of Life and Death in Medieval English Literature* (New York: New York Univ. Press, 1976), pp. 152-83.

10. Possibly the earliest reference to knowledge of death through such a figure standing beside a person is recorded in 1151; the sacristan of Saint-Paul-de-Narbonne, according to an inscription at the Musée des Augustines in Toulouse (No. 855) reported by Philippe Ariès, *The Hour of Our Death*, trans. Helen Weaver (New York: Knopf, 1981), pp. 6-7, "saw death standing beside him and knew that he was about to die."

11. Chambers, *Population, Economy, and Society*, pp. 84-85.

12. Giovanni Boccaccio, *The Decameron*, trans. Mark Musa and Peter E. Bondanella (New York: Norton, 1977), p. 3.

13. V. Pritchard, *English Medieval Graffiti* (Cambridge: Cambridge Univ. Press, 1967), p. 182.

14. The banner, now in the Mansell Collection, is from Perugia, and is dated 1464. A large figure of the Virgin stands above, with her mantle spread out to protect her followers. Prominent saints stand around her, and the angels prepare to do battle; below, St. Raphael aims a dart at Death himself, who stands over those he has slain. The Virgin as a protector of souls is a frequent motif in English and continental iconography. See the continental *Speculum Humanae Salvationis*, for example, in Codex San-Florianensis XI, 148A, fol. 252, where she is shown protecting souls with her mantle (color microfilm available at Hill Monastic Manuscript Library). An earlier manuscript, Bodleian MS. Laud. Misc. 469, which contains St. Augustine's *City of God*, shows the Virgin Mary actively taking part in a struggle for the soul of man, which she is holding out to an angel that will take it up to heaven. See C. M. Kaufmann, *Romanesque Manuscripts 1066-1190* (London: Harvey Miller, 1975), No. 54.

15. William Benham, *Old St. Paul's Cathedral* (London: Seeley, 1902), p. 10; William Dugdale, *The History of St. Pauls Cathedral in London* (London, 1658), pp. 131-32; James M. Clark, *The Dance of Death in the Middle Ages and the Renaissance* (Glasgow: Jackson, 1950), pp. 7-21.

16. Florence Warren, ed., *The Dance of Death*, EETS, o.s. 181 (1931), pp. xxi-xxiii.

17. Examples in the visual arts in England are all relatively late; these

NOTES

include the misericords from St. George's Chapel, Windsor, and those (now lost) from St. Michael's Cathedral, Coventry (see Remnant, *Catalogue*, p. 7, and Mary Dormer Harris, "The Misericords of Coventry," *Transactions of the Birmingham Archaeological Society*, 52 [1927], 262-63, Pl. XXXI), as well as painted glass from St. Andrew's, Norwich (fig. 22; see also George A. King, "The Pre-Reformation Painted Glass in St. Andrew's Church, Norwich," *Norfolk Archaeology*, 18 [1913], 291-93) and the very fragmentary wall painting under paneling in the Guild Chapel at Stratford-upon-Avon (Wilfrid Puddephat, "The Mural Paintings of the Dance of Death in the Guild Chapel of Stratford-upon-Avon," *Transactions of the Birmingham Archaeological Society*, 76 [1960], 29-35, and Clifford Davidson, *The Guild Chapel Wall Paintings at Stratford-upon-Avon* [New York: AMS Press, 1988], pp. 6-7). For additional discussion of later examples, see Chew, *Pilgrimage of Life*, pp. 226-46. Some further items are noted by Clark, *Dance of Death*, pp. 7-21.

18. *Dance of Death*, ed. Warren, p. 7.

19. *Ludus Coventriae*, ed. Block, pp. 173-77.

20. Some early representations of Death are conveniently published in Dietrich Briesemeister, *Bilder des Todes* (Unterschneidheim, 1970), and Levin et al., *Images of Love and Death*, Pls. XXXV-LXVIII.

21. Harris, "Misericords of Coventry," pp. 262-63, Pl. XXXI.

22. See King, "The Pre-Reformation Painted Glass," pp. 291-93.

23. The figures on the title pages of Skot's two undated editions of *Everyman* are made up from separate woodcuts representing the young man and Death; for commentary, see Clifford Davidson, "Of Woodcut and Play," *EDAM Newsletter*, 3, No. 2 (1981), 14-17. For another illustration of Death coming to a representative man in drama, see Chaundler, *Liber Apologeticus*, ed. Shoukri, Pl. 13.

24. Worcester Cathedral Library MS. F. 10, fol. 48^v, as quoted by Owst, *Literature and Pulpit*, p. 528.

25. Gibson, "East Anglian Drama and the Dance of Death," p. 6.

26. Kathleen Cohen, *Metamorphosis of a Death Symbol: The Transi Tomb in the Late Middle Ages and the Renaissance* (Berkeley and Los Angeles: Univ. of California Press, 1973), fig. 13. For a parallel in manuscript illumination, see British Library MS. Add. 37,049, fol. 32^v, as reproduced in Marjorie M. Malvern, "An Earnest 'monyscyon' and 'thinge delectabyll' Realized Verbally and Visually in 'A Disputacion betwyx the Body and Wormes,' a Middle English Poem Inspired by Tomb Art and Northern Spirituality," *Viator*, 13 (1982), fig. 1.

27. Significantly, the Dance of Death as illustrated in the misericords

NOTES

in St. Michael's Cathedral, Coventry, was linked with the Corporal Acts of Mercy; see Harris, "Misericords of Coventry," pp. 262-63.

28. *Two Tudor Interludes: The Interlude of Youth, Hick Scorner*, ed. Ian Lancashire (Baltimore: Johns Hopkins Univ. Press, 1980), p. 233.

29. *Non-Cycle Plays and Fragments*, ed. Norman Davis, EETS, s.s. 1 (1970), pp. lxxxv-lxxxvi, c; Bevington, "'Blake and wyght, fowll and fayer'," pp. 136-37.

30. See, for example, Sixten Ringbom, "*Maria in Sole* and the Virgin of the Rosary," *Journal of the Warburg and Courtauld Institutes*, 25 (1962), 326-30.

31. There is extensive iconographic evidence for embalming; see, for example, the figures of Louis XII and his queen at Saint-Denis (Boase, *Death in the Middle Ages*, fig. 86). Cf. Edelgard DuBruck, *The Theme of Death in French Poetry of the Middle Ages and the Renaissance* (The Hague: Mouton, 1964), p. 51, and also Elizabeth A. R. Brown, "Death and the Human Body in the Later Middle Ages: The Legislation of Boniface VIII on the Division of the Corpse," *Viator*, 12 (1981), 221-70.

32. Such attitudes were even reflected in population statistics, which show a leveling off of the population in Europe approximately sixty years before the great plague of 1348-49; see Chambers, *Population, Economy, and Society*, pp. 19-20.

33. Davis, ed., *Non-Cycle Plays and Fragments*, pp. lxxxv-lxxxvi.

34. See Douglas Gray, *Themes and Images in the Medieval English Religious Lyric* (London: Routledge and Kegan Paul, 1972), pp. 208-09; Raimond van Marle, *Iconographie de l'art profane et à la Renaissance* (1931; rpt. New York: Hacker, 1971), I, 383-95.

35. Willy F. Storck, "Aspects of Death in English Art and Poetry--II," *Burlington Magazine*, 21 (1912), 314-19.

36. See also Storck, "Aspects of Death," p. 319. For another example, see especially Wensley Church in Yorkshire, which has a wall painting of c.1330 with the following inscriptions placed perpendicularly between the figures which are the dead: "[As] we a[re] nove [...] [Thus] sal the be [...] [B]ewar wyt me"; see Tristram, *English Wall Painting of the Fourteenth Century*, p. 262.

37. Pritchard, *English Medieval Graffiti*, p. 44.

38. Kathi Meyer-Baer, *Music of the Spheres and the Dance of Death* (Princeton: Princeton Univ. Press, 1970), pp. 294, 296.

39. This figure of the fashionably dressed person is repeated in the edition of c.1530 on the verso of the title page; here he appears along with Fellowship, Beauty, Discretion, Kindred, and Strength. See Davidson,

NOTES

"Of Woodcut and Play," p. 15.

40. Ruth Caspar, "'All Shall Be Well': Prototypical Symbols of Hope," *Journal of the History of Ideas*, 42 (1981), 139-40.

41. See V. A. Kolve, "*Everyman* and the Parable of the Talents," in *Medieval Drama*, ed. Taylor and Nelson, pp. 316-40, for comment on this aspect of the play's meaning.

42. See Dutka, *Music in the English Mystery Plays*, pp. 47-50.

43. Davidson and O'Connor, *York Art*, p. 112.

44. See also Jeffrey, "Franciscan Spirituality and the Rise of Early English Drama," pp. 26-27.

45. *Dance of Death*, ed. Warren, p. 49.

1. Sower and Seed. Painted glass. North Choir Aisle, Canterbury Cathedral. (Photograph: Royal Commission on the Historical Monuments of England.)

2. Wife beating husband. Misericord, Chester Cathedral. (Photograph: Conway Library, Courtauld Institute of Art; by permission of Fred H. Crossley and Maurice H. Ridgway.)

3. Demon Fool with limp club before King. Oxford, Bodleian Library MS. Don. d. 85, fol. 35^v.

4. Fool dances, with King turned away from him to Deity. British Library MS. Harley 2897, fol. 42^v. (By permission of the British Library.)

5. Adam digs while Eve spins; center, Expulsion of Adam and Eve from Eden. Misericord, Ely Cathedral. (Photograph: Royal Commission on the Historical Monuments of England.)

6. Detail of Doom showing Devil with mouth shaped like anus. Painted glass, West Window, Church of St. Mary, Fairford. (Photograph: Royal Commission on the Historical Monuments of England.)

7. Fall of Lucifer. Fallen angels, in process of transformation into devils. Painted glass, Church of St. Michael, Spurriergate, York.

8. Tutivillus. Bench end, Church of St. Mary the Virgin, Charlton Mackrel, Somerset. (Photograph: Royal Commission on the Historical Monuments of England.)

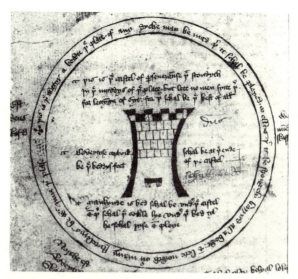

9. Staging diagram for *The Castle of Perseverance*. Macro Manuscript (Folger Shakespeare Library MS. V.a.354). (By permission of the Folger Shakespeare Library.)

10. Wise and Foolish Virgins. Painted glass, Church of St. Mary, Melbury Bubb, Dorset. (Photograph: Royal Commission on the Historical Monuments of England.)

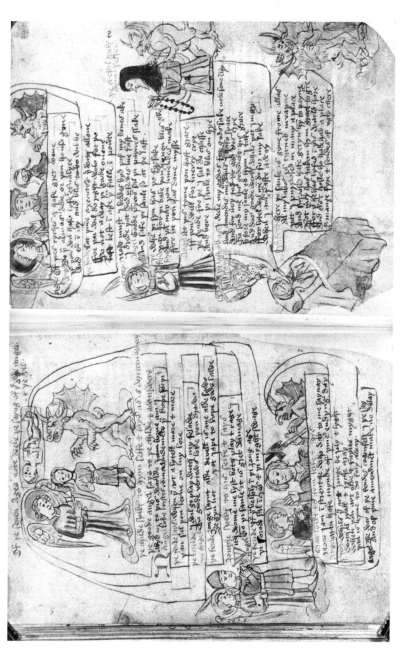

11. The Ages of Man. British Library Add. MS. 37,049, fols. 28ᵛ–29. (By permission of the British Library.)

12. Wheel of Fortune. Wall painting, Rochester Cathedral. (Photograph: Royal Commission on the Historical Monuments of England.)

13. The Fortified Castle. Master of La Forteresse de la Foy. Vienna, Österreichische Nationalbibliothek, Cod. 2536, fol. 15.

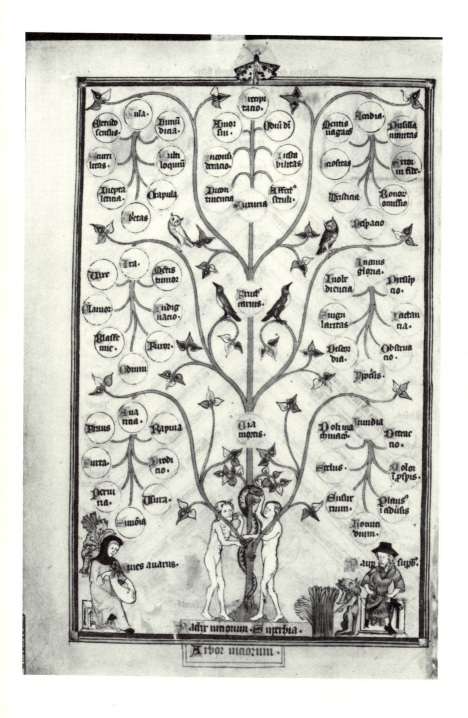

14. Tree of Vices. Robert de Lisle Psalter. British Library MS. Arundel 83. (By permission of the British Library.)

15. Attack on Castle defended by Ladies. Ivory Mirror Case. Victoria and Albert Museum. (By courtesy of the Board of Trustees of the Victoria and Albert Museum.)

16. Attack on Castle defended by Ladies. Luttrell Psalter. British Library MS. Add. 42,130, fol. 75^v. (By permission of the British Library.)

17. Last Judgment, with Seven Deadly Sins and Corporal Acts of Mercy. Wall painting, Trotton, Sussex. (Photograph: Royal Commission on the Historical Monuments of England.)

18. Souls being carried to Hell by Demons. Painted Glass, West Window, Church of St. Mary, Fairford. (Photograph: Royal Commission on the Historical Monuments of England.)

19. Wheel of Life. Robert de Lisle Psalter. British Library, MS. Arundel 83, fol. 126ᵛ. (By permission of the British Library.)

21. Seven Sacraments font showing Absolution. Church of St. Andrew, Westhall, Suffolk. (Photograph: Royal Commission on the Historical Monuments of England.)

20. Synagogue. Font, Church of St. Peter, Southrop, Gloucestershire. (Photograph: Royal Commission on the Historical Monuments of England.)

22. Death comes for the Bishop, from a Dance of Death series. Painted glass, St. Andrew's, Norwich.

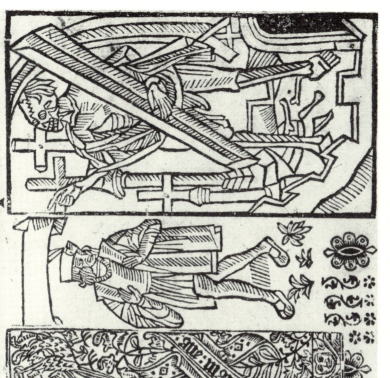

23. Death and *Everyman*. Title page from undated edition of Everyman issued by Skot (c.1530). (By permission of the Huntington Library.)

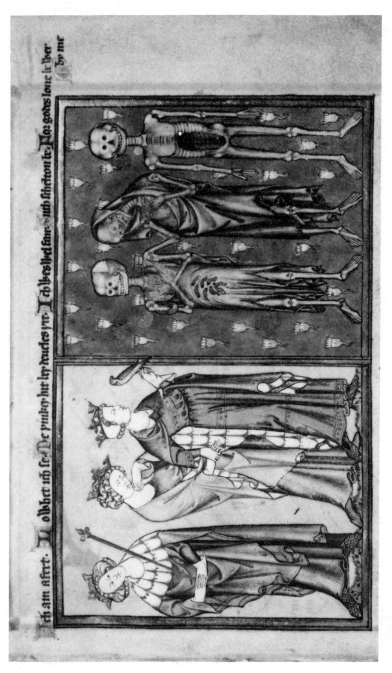

24. The Three Living and the Three Dead. Robert de Lisle Psalter. British Library MS. Arundel 83, fol. 127. (By permission of the British Library.)

Index

Abel 70
Accidia, Sloth 9, 39
Adam 6, 21, 29-30, 56, 97, 100, 122, fig. 5
Adams, Joseph Quincy 33
Ages of Man 50, 53-55, 146, 156-57, fig. 11
Ambrose, St. 121
Amiens 65
angels, good and evil 55-58, 60
Apocalypse 41
Apollonia, St. 141
Aquinas, St. Thomas 7
Ars Moriendi 127
Ashley, Kathleen 9, 142
Ashwell, graffito at 117
Augustine, St. 93, 97, 104-05, 156, 160

Bardwell, wall painting at 75
Barlow Psalter 27, 41
Basil, St. 60
Beadle, Richard 50, 133, 145
Beatniffe, Richard 131
Bennett, Jacob 132
Bernard, St., of Clairvaux 24, 93
Beverley Minster, misericord at 26
Bevington, David 9, 11, 13, 34, 83, 131
Biblia Pauperum 158
Billington, Sandra 140
Blythburgh, benchend at 75
Boccaccio 116
Boethius 132
Bosch, Hieronymus 75, 77

British Library, MS. Add. 24,199 57-58; MS. Add. 25,698 43; Harley MS. 2897 (Psalter) 26
British Museum, ivory in 13
Bury St. Edmunds 1-3, 26, 83, 118, 130, 132-34

Cain 70
Canterbury Cathedral, painted glass in 17, 29-30, fig. 1; wall painting at 85, 89; tomb at 121
Capgrave, John 145
Carpenter, Sarah 153
Castle of Perseverance 1-4, 6-7, 10-12, 20, 24, 47-82, 83, 116, 118-19, 121, 124-25, 129, 132, 145, fig. 9
Caviness, Madeline 17
Charlton Mackrell, benchend at 36, fig. 2
Chaundler, Thomas 152
Chichele, Henry, tomb of 121-22
Chester 87; Cathedral, misericord at 29, fig. 2
Chicester Cathedral 26
Christ 11, 16, 19, 21-22, 26-27, 35, 61-62, 65, 67, 81, 84, 87-90, 97, 103, 107-10, 119-20, 154-55
Clopper, Lawrence 9
Coleridge, Samuel T. 6-7
Coletti, Theresa 155
Collier, John Payne 4-5
Conrad of Hirsau 69
Corporal Acts of Mercy 17, 20, 22-23, 41, 70-71, 75, 139, 162

INDEX

Council of Nicea 87
Coventry 87; St. Michael's Cathedral, misericords at 120, 161
Craig, Hardin 8
Crostwright 75

Dance of Death 49, 76, 80, 104, 115, 118-22, 126, 130, 161, fig. 22
Davenport, W. A. 84, 136, 144
David, St. 18
De Lisle Psalter 66, 97, 126, 149, 151, figs. 14, 19, 24
de Massa, Michael 89
Devil's dance 102, 130, 157
Digby plays 1, 24, 40, 63, 103, 105, 133-34, 140
Dublin, Priory of Holy Trinity at 126

Eccles, Mark 9-10, 95, 138, 158
Edmund, St. 132, *frontispiece*
Edwards, John 137
Egmont Psalter 77
Ely Cathedral, misericord in 30, 36, fig. 5
Eve 21, 30, 56, 100
Everyman 8, 11, 114-15, 118, 120-25, 127-29

Fairford, parish church, misericord in 29, 34; painted glass at 79, 152, figs. 6, 18
Farnham, Willard 114
Folger Shakespeare Library, MS. V.a.354 2, fig. 9
fool 26-28, 41-43, 59, figs. 3-4
Forteresse de la Foy, La 63, fig. 13

Fortune 58-59, fig. 12
Fountain of Life 21-22
Fouquet, Jean 141
Four Daughters of God 20, 47-48, 76, 79-81, 129, 152
Friedsam Annunciation 95
Furnivall, Frederick 10

Gamlingay 127
Garner, Stanton, Jr. 134
Ghent 66; painting in cathedral at 21
Gibson, Gail McMurray 83, 121, 132-33
Giotto 43
Gloria 17
Glossa ordinaria 158
Green, Joseph 88
Green, Rosalie 148
Gregory the Great, St. 32
Grosseteste, Robert 80
Gurney, Hudson 1, 131
Gylliot, John 129

Happé, Peter 83, 157
hell 78-79, 81, 130, fig. 18
Henry VI, King 4
Henry VII, Chapel of, at Westminster Abbey, misericord in 28
Herod 119, 127-28
Hick Scorner 8, 123
Hildegard of Bingen 67, 158
Hill, Eugene D. 11, 93
Hilton, Walter 88, 92
Holbein, Hans 120, 122
Holkham Bible Picture Book 30, 78-79
Hone, William 4
Hortus Deliciarum, by Herrad of Landsberg 64

INDEX

Hoxne, wall painting at 70, 75
Hugh of St.-Victor 24
Huizinga, J. 115
Huth Psalter 107
Hyngham, Thomas 2, 132, *frontispiece*

Image of Pity 89-90
Ingatestone, wall painting at 39, 58

Jacob's Well 35-36, 96
Jerusalem 106-07
Jesse 81
Job 32-35, 37, 141-42
John of Damascus, St. 93-94
John the Baptist, St. 19, 155
John the Evangelist, St. 155
Jonson, Ben 147
Johnston, Alexandra F. 153
Judas 42-43, 70
Julian of Norwich 114

Kelley, Michael R. 136
Kempe, Margery 110, 114

Lambeth Bible 81
Lamentations 106
Lancashire, Ian 135
Laon 65
Liber Floridus 66
Lindenbaum, Sheila 136
Little, Lester K. 151
Logos 11, 84, 88
London 30; St. Paul's Cathedral, cloisters with Dance of Death 117-18, 120
Longhurst, Margaret H. 149
Long Melford, painted glass at 132, *frontispiece*; tomb at 121

Longthorpe Tower, wall painting at 55, 97, 138
Louis XII, King of France 162
Lucifer 34, 96, 99-100, 124, fig. 7
Luttrell Psalter 67, 73, fig. 16
Lydgate, John 118, 120, 130

Mackenzie, Roy 8, 10
Macro, Cox 1, 4, 131
Mâle, Émile 39, 115
Mankind 1-2, 5-6, 8-10, 15-45, 83, 109, 123-24, 138
Marlowe, Christopher 56, 100, 143
Mary, Blessed Virgin 30-31, 42, 63, 81, 87, 108, 117, 125, 160
Mary Magdalene, Digby play 24, 63, 103, 140
Mary Magdalene 40, 63, 105
May, Steven 141
McCutchan, J. Wilson 151
Meditations on the Life of Christ 79
Medwall, Henry 8, 95, 114
Melbury Bubb, painted glass at 40, fig. 10
Mephostophilis 100
Michael, St. 79
Milton, John 8
Mirk, John 38, 63
Molloy, John J. 106
More, St. Thomas 114-15

Nagler, A. M. 137
Naples, catacomb art at 67
Neuss, Paula 9, 34, 40
Nigra sum 96
Nilus the Scholastic 86
Northmoor, wall painting at 147
Norwich 1; St. Andrew's church, painted glass in 120, 161, fig. 22

INDEX

Nottingham Castle Museum, alabaster at 85-86
Novem virtutes 88, 158
N-town cycle 1, 80, 119, 127-28
Nyborg, Ebbe 142

"Of the Seven Ages" 54-56, 78
Oil of Mercy 97-98
Ormesby Psalter 27
Owst, G. R. 115

Packwood, wall painting at 126
Padua, Arena Chapel 43
Panofsky, Erwin 7
Parry, David 145
Pater Noster play 7
Patteson, John 131
Paul, St. 24, 109
Penrith, round at 51
Perugia, banner from 160
Peter, St. 23, 70
Peterborough Psalter 27-28, 68
Pickering, F. P. 13
Piehler, Paul 6
Pierpont Morgan Library, Book of Hours 81
Plato 56
Pollard, A. W. 8, 10, 136
Porphyry 154
Potter, Robert 6, 11, 158
Pride of Life, The 8, 12, 124-27
Prudentius 10, 24, 32, 64, 140, 158

Ramsay Psalter 155
Raphael, St. 160
Records of Early English Drama 131, 145
Riehle, Wolfgang 110
Riggio, Milla Cozart 11, 47, 76-77, 154

Ripple, misericord at 18
Robert of Brunne 36
Rochester Cathedral, wall painting at 58, fig. 12
Rolle, Richard 88, 114

St.-Denis 162
St. Martial of Limoges, *Sponsus* from 39
St. Neots, painted glass at 97
Salisbury Cathedral, sculptures at 64-65, 69
Sarum Missal 96
Sarum rite 17, 23
Satan 94
Sawles Warde 67
Saxl, Frtiz 147
Schell, Edgar 146
Schmitt, Natalie Crohn 6, 95, 145
Schongauer, Martin 39
Seasons, representations of 18, 138-39
Seth 97
Seven Deadly Sins 7, 24, 39-41, 51, 54, 58-59, 61-64, 71-72, 75, 80, 105, 148, fig. 17
Shakespeare, William 59, 92, 94
Sharp, Thomas 4
Sheingorn, Pamela 133, 155
Shepherd of Hermas 57, 67
Sidney, Sir Philip 150
Sidney Sussex College, MS. 76 27
Skot, John 121, 127, 161, fig. 23
Southampton 116
Southern, Richard 3, 52, 63, 137-38, 141, 146
Southrop 107, fig. 20
Speculum humanae salvationis 141-42, 144, 160
Speculum Sacerdotale 22-23

168

INDEX

Speculum virginum 69
Spenser, Edmund 8, 32, 43
Spivack, Bernard 95
Strasbourg Cathedral, sculpture at 150
Stratford-upon-Avon, wall paintings at 150, 161
Suso, Henry 88, 90

Te Deum 17, 82
Thompson, E. N. S. 10
Three Enemies of Man 7, 23-24, 48, 54, 57-59, 98, fig. 8
Three Living and Three Dead 126, fig. 24
Titivillus 18, 23-24, 31, 34-38, fig. 8
Tota pulcra es 96
Towneley plays 25, 35, 82, 141
Tree of Vice (*Arbor mala*) 66, 70, 75, fig. 14
Tree of Virtue (*Arbor bona*) 66
Trinity 18, 81, 88, 98, 110, 154
Tristram, E. W. 138, 143, 148
Trotton, wall painting at 71, 75, 139, 148, fig. 17
Turner, Victor 87
Twycross, Meg 153

Uppsala Cathedral, corbels at 65

van Eyck, Jan 23, 108
van Leyden, Lucas 103
Victoria and Albert Museum, ivory in 67; embroidery in 85; mirror case in 149, fig. 15
Veni, electa mei 128
Virtues and Vices 32, 54, 63-66, 72-75
Virtues, iconography of 66-71

Wager, W. 109
Walsham-le-Willows, theater at 50, 145
Warton, Thomas 5, 8
Wasson, John 133
Wells Cathedral, sculpture at 25, 33
Wensley, wall painting at 162
Wentersdorf, Karl 142
Wenzel, Siegfried 23, 38-39, 52
Westhall, font at 109, fig. 21
Westminster Abbey, misericord in 28
Wheel of Life *fig.* 19
Wheel of Senses 97
Williams, Arnold 10
Winchelsea, wall painting at 147
Windsor, St. George's Chapel, misericords at 161
Wisdom 1-2, 4, 10-11, 83-111, 129, 133-34, 153, 155, 158
Wise and Foolish Virgins 39, 96, fig. 10
Woodforde, Christopher 1

York 86-87
York, All Saints, North Street, woodcarving at 129
York, Holy Trinity Goodramgate, painted glass at 85
York Minster, painted glass in 44; sculpture at 152; painted ceiling from chapter house 107
York, St. Michael, Spurriergate, painted glass in 34, fig. 7
Yorkshire Museum, tympanum at 56